ROUTLEDGE LIBRARY EDITIONS:
SEMANTICS AND SEMIOLOGY

Volume 11

WORD MEANING AND BELIEF

WORD MEANING AND BELIEF

S. G. PULMAN

LONDON AND NEW YORK

First published in 1983 by Croom Helm Ltd

This edition first published in 2017
by Routledge
2 Park Square, Milton Park, Abingdon, Oxon OX14 4RN

and by Routledge
711 Third Avenue, New York, NY 10017

Routledge is an imprint of the Taylor & Francis Group, an informa business

© 1983 S. G. Pulman

All rights reserved. No part of this book may be reprinted or reproduced or utilised in any form or by any electronic, mechanical, or other means, now known or hereafter invented, including photocopying and recording, or in any information storage or retrieval system, without permission in writing from the publishers.

Trademark notice: Product or corporate names may be trademarks or registered trademarks, and are used only for identification and explanation without intent to infringe.

British Library Cataloguing in Publication Data
A catalogue record for this book is available from the British Library

ISBN: 978-1-138-69750-8 (Set)
ISBN: 978-1-315-52029-2 (Set) (ebk)
ISBN: 978-1-138-69048-6 (Volume 11) (hbk)
ISBN: 978-1-138-69052-3 (Volume 11) (pbk)
ISBN: 978-1-315-53689-7 (Volume 11) (ebk)

Publisher's Note
The publisher has gone to great lengths to ensure the quality of this reprint but points out that some imperfections in the original copies may be apparent.

Disclaimer
The publisher has made every effort to trace copyright holders and would welcome correspondence from those they have been unable to trace.

Word Meaning and Belief

S.G. PULMAN

CROOM HELM
London & Canberra

© 1983 S.G. Pulman
Croom Helm Ltd, Provident House, Burrell Row,
Beckenham, Kent BR3 1AT

British Library Cataloguing in Publication Data

Pulman, S.G.
   Word meaning and belief. – (Croom Helm linguistics series)
   1. Word (Linguistics)
   I. Title
   418'.01   P245
   ISBN 0-7099-2035-0

Printed and bound in Great Britain
by Billing & Sons Limited, Worcester.

CONTENTS

Preface

1.	The Possibility of a Theory of Word Meaning	9
2.	Against Semantic Primitives	29
3.	Naïve Metaphysics	52
4.	Theories of Categorisation	83
5.	Verbs, Prototypes and Family Resemblances	107
6.	Semantic Categories	137
Bibliography		170
Index		178

PREFACE

As a linguist, it was somewhat depressing to discover that the most interesting work on word meaning seemed to be taking place not in linguistics, but in philosophy and psychology. Although (as will no doubt be evident), I have no special qualifications in these fields it seemed a worthwhile project to try to investigate the linguistic implications of this work, and in particular, to try to integrate it within the general methodological framework of generative grammar. In part, then, this book is an attempt at such a synthesis. But to do this involved some rethinking about the scope of a theory of word meaning and its relationship with some of the preoccupations of recent work in these other disciplines. So I have also tried to provide some kind of alternative to the, to my mind, unsatisfactory current approaches within linguistics. The outline presented here is limited: it does not deal with all types of words and it does not deal to any significant extent with the interaction of such a theory with the formal semantic or pragmatic (or syntactic) description of languages. However, I hope it will prove substantial enough to be the basis for further work.

The structure of the book is as follows: Chapters 1 and 2 are methodological preliminaries, discussing Quine's objections to the feasibility of a theory of word meaning, and criticising attempts to answer these objections on the basis of postulated universal semantic primitives. Chapter 3 provides a by no means exhaustive list of desiderata for a theory of word meaning: that it should provide (1) a definition of a naturally 'nameable thing', (2) an account of the principles of categorisation by which different things can be grouped together and designated by the same term and (3) a description of the 'semantic categories' or semantically significant groupings of words found in a language. The first of these requirements is discussed in the remainder of that chapter, the second in Chapters 4 and 5 and the third in Chapter 6.

Some of the material in Chapter 2 is adapted from my PhD thesis for the University of Essex (1977) and I thank Martin Atkinson, John Lyons and Yorick Wilks for their comments on that. Parts of Chapters 5 and 6 have been given as talks at various universities and I am grateful to the audiences on these occasions for their suggestions, as well as to

Preface

the students and colleagues who helped carry out the experiments reported in Chapter 5. Patrick Griffiths also gave me many helpful comments on that chapter: Alan Cruse, Jim Hurford and Graeme Ritchie read a complete earlier draft and likewise gave me many valuable comments.

1 THE POSSIBILITY OF A THEORY OF WORD MEANING

I

A necessary starting point for any book dealing with the topic of a theory of word meaning is the attack mounted by Quine against the very possibility of such a theory, at least in any scientifically respectable form.[1] Quine's arguments are persuasive and his pessimistic view continues to be extremely influential among philosophers of language (for example, Davidson 1973, 1974a; Putnam 1978), and some linguists (Sampson 1980), though, as we might expect, not among all (Katz 1975; Chomsky 1976, 1980). Although many linguists are tempted to follow Katz in regarding Quine's objections as merely the legacy of a discredited behaviourism, it seems to me that he cannot be written off quite so easily, and that we can learn something quite important by taking his objections seriously and attempting to answer them.

Quine's attack focuses on two related concepts, the 'meaning' of a sentence and the idea of a 'correct' translation. As regards the first, his argument goes roughly like this: to ask for the meaning of a sentence is misguided since it suggests that there is a thing — a meaning — associated with a sentence but possibly independent of it. This meaning might perhaps have been expressed by another sentence of the same language or by a sentence of a different language. This, he says, is at best misleading, for sentences are not understood in isolation, but in virtue of their place in the language, their relationship with other sentences. It is therefore impossible to isolate an individual sentence and ask for its meaning, for its meaning is partly concerned with its implicit relationships with other sentences of the language. Quine sees an analogy here between this point and the observation that, in general, scientific theories do not stand or fall by specific individual predictions, but by an overall confrontation with experience. This is part of a wider analogy between language and theories, and our understanding of both, according to Quine, must be 'holistic'.

To moderate the search for meanings to a search for equivalence of meaning or synonymy is no answer to this objection, for it is to be subscribing to the doctrine that there is an analytic-synthetic distinction; a doctrine that some sentences are true or false simply because of what they mean, while others are true or false because of the way the world is. Quine shows convincingly that there is a logical connection between the concepts of meaning, synonymy and analyticity, and that they form a circle which there is no way of breaking into or out of. No one of these concepts is more basic than the others. Quine concedes that it is perhaps harmless to talk of analyticity with respect to formal tautologies or explicitly defined notations, but that as regards the non-logical contributions to sentences, there is no distinction of principle between synonymy and widely shared belief. Thus if the hackneyed examples:

(1)   Joe is a bachelor
(2)   Joe is a man who has never married

are judged to mean the same, that is because our beliefs about bachelors are included in or identical to our beliefs about unmarried men. Similarly for so-called analytic sentences: if

(3)   Cats are animals

is true, it is true (trivially) because we have just so defined cat (partially) or (more interestingly), because our beliefs about animals include the belief that cats are an instance of the natural kind 'animal': this belief is based on other beliefs about the make up of cats and the (probably inexplicit) criteria for being an animal. So (3) is judged to be true (or even necessarily true) not just because we believe that cats are animals, but because to overturn that belief would entail a fairly radical revision of many of our other beliefs about living, mobile creatures. In this respect (3) is unlike (4):

(4)   There are ten countries in the European Economic Community

which would require relatively little perturbation of our total system of beliefs to imagine it being false.[2] However, this distinction is one of degree rather than of kind, even though the discrepancy in the number of relevant beliefs (or differences in distance from the centre of our belief system, to use a spatial metaphor), may provide us with an intuition that the distinction is one of principle.

It follows from this view of how words have significance that the process of understanding a speaker of our own, or another, language is in part a process of attributing to him beliefs which make sense of his uttering certain sentences in certain situations. In order to get started at this game we have to assume rationality on the part of others – that the aim of using language as far as truth and falsity are concerned is to speak truly, on the whole, not falsely. We also have to aim for the maximisation of the consistency of the beliefs we are attributing, even if this means that occasionally we may come across sentences where we disagree over truth value. For example, in trying to understand an alien language, when we have reached the stage of being able to talk fluently about everyday life, we would, on translating some utterance as 'beans are the souls of dead ancestors' be inclined to attribute to the speaker a peculiar, to us false, belief rather than adjust our translation of 'beans', 'dead', 'soul' or 'ancestors', since by hypothesis, we seem to agree with him over these words when used elsewhere.

Much of this may seem rather remote from the concerns of linguists but the general idea is familiar from a discussion in a rather different context. McCawley (1971:219) is making precisely the same point when he argues that someone who utters in all sincerity:

(5) My toothbrush is alive and is trying to kill me

'should be referred to a psychiatric clinic and not to a remedial English course' (for a lesson on selectional restrictions). The reason is that in order to assume that the speaker is saying what he believes to be the truth, we have to attribute to him beliefs which for a member of our society are taken as evidence of mental illness. Thus the same problem over what to make of 'beans are the souls of dead ancestors' can arise within a language as well as across languages.

In some cases, though, we might decide that the speaker is using some words differently from us. Consider the case (from Davidson, 1969) where someone says, apparently sincerely,

(6) There's a hippopotamus in the fridge.

Does he mean what we would mean by those words? Perhaps; but if he were to continue with 'It's yellow and round, and I propose we cut it in two, sprinkle sugar on it and eat it up for breakfast' then we would be more inclined to think that he means by 'hippopotamus' what we mean by 'grapefruit', always assuming we think he agrees with us on 'yellow' and 'round', etc. These are deliberately striking cases where the discrepancies are obvious. But in other cases there may be no clear and determinate answer. As Davidson puts it:

> Hesitation over whether to translate a saying of another by one or another of various non-synonymous sentences of mine does not necessarily reflect a lack of information: it is just that beyond a certain point there is no deciding even in principle between the view that the Other has used words as we do but has more or less weird beliefs and the view that we have translated him wrong. (pp. 137-8)

In the real world we do not find:

> the sharpness questions of meaning must in principle have if meanings are entities. (*op. cit.*)

Since there are no such entities as meanings which different sentences can express, there can be no such things as fully determinate radical translation from another language. Quine puts the matter in this way:

> There is the stubborn notion that we can tell intuitively which idea someone's sentence expresses, our sentence anyway, even when the intuition is irreducible to behavioural criteria. This is why one thinks that one's question 'What did the native say?' has a right answer independently of choices among mutually incompatible manuals of translation. (1969:276)

II

The above is Quine's celebrated thesis of the 'indeterminacy of translation'. In exploring it, Quine invites us to consider a hypothetical linguist engaged in producing a translation manual for some unknown language which he does not speak yet and whose speakers do not speak English or any other language known to him. (As will become clear, Quine's linguist operates under severe methodological restrictions, and his bible is Harris's (1951) *Methods in Structural Linguistics*.) First of all he notices that certain sounds are used in the presence of certain things and by suitable gestures and profferings he arrives at the words for what in English are called, say, 'tree', 'person', 'rabbit' and so on. By processes of substitution and comparison he arrives at the phonology, morphology and syntax of the language. Simple 'occasion sentences' whose 'stimulus meanings' (apparently regular applicability to certain observable things) vary negligibly between speakers are labelled 'observation sentences'. These are sentences that the linguist would be inclined to translate as 'this is a tree', 'this is a rabbit' and so on. Being conscientious about his methodology, our linguist justifies his inclination to translate these sentences in this way by attributing to the speakers of the language an implicit ontological framework: for example that they distinguish a class of physical objects in much the same way as we do, that this class contains subclasses which can be labelled 'animate' and 'inanimate', etc.: such an attribution is an 'analytic hypothesis' which among other similar hypotheses helps to make sense of the observation sentences: why something cannot be called both a tree and a rabbit, for example. The completed translation manual consists of a syntax, a dictionary derived from observation sentences, and a set of analytical hypotheses (as well as morphological and phonological information).

Observation sentences, says Quine, suffer from the ordinary kind of inductive uncertainty associated with any hypothesis which goes beyond the available data: future observations might show, for example, that the stimulus meaning for a particular sentence did diverge across speakers at certain points. But analytical hypotheses suffer from a different and deeper kind of uncertainty, namely that it does not even make sense to ask whether a particular system of hypotheses is right or wrong. For any system which is consistent with the observation sentences there will always be rival systems equally consistent with the observation sentences but not necessarily compatible with each other, or with the original system. So, to use Quine's own example, 'gavagai' would be translated as 'rabbit' on the analytic hypothesis that speakers of the language had the same concept of individual objects as we do. For us, objects have parts, not the other way round: the semantically basic member of the pair *part/whole* is *whole*. For example, we say of the shape ○ that it is a circle and that ⌒ is a circle with a part missing. We do not say that ⌒ ∪ ⌒ etc. are shmircles, and that ○ is a shmircle with all its parts. Though it appears in fact that no language countenances such a lexical structure, it is by no means impossible to conceive of people who could manage such a system. So there would be no logical problem encountered if we decided to adopt the analytic hypothesis that for our alien language the basic term of *part/whole* was *part*: in other words, that the speakers of the language had a somewhat different conception of objects from ourselves. On this hypothesis, 'gavagai' should be translated as 'rabbit parts attached to each other' or as Quine has it, 'undetached rabbit part'. Alternatively, we might hypothesise that stability over time was not one of the factors involved in the notion of a physical object for our speakers, although it is for us. And so our translation of 'gavagai' might be 'there is rabbiting now', or Quine's 'Lo, rabbithood again'.

The point of all this is not to deny that we have intuitions that some of these analytical hypotheses are simpler or more plausible than others, for we do, but to stress that there is no basis, either empirical or in logic, for these intuitions: what we see as the 'unnaturalness' of some of these translations is merely due to a parochial preference for our own ontological framework. However, all the other hypotheses will fit the facts equally well (we assume) and so the question as to which system is correct is unanswerable (or unaskable). There is no 'fact of the matter' to decide between them: all are equally valid from a logical point of view.

Although this rather brief and selective discussion does not do full justice to Quine's overall position, it will be seen how easily his arguments lead to pessimism about the possibility of a respectable theory of word meaning. If semantics is the study of meanings, it has nothing to study, since there are no meanings attached to sentences in the way they have traditionally been conceived. If semantics is the study of translation, and aims to construct translation manuals for particular languages and thence to construct a theory of translation manuals, then it is again doomed as a scientific enterprise (though not necessarily a practical one) since apparently it must admit an unacceptable degree of indeterminacy, in effect, that is, having no criteria for success or failure.

III

There are several kinds of response which the linguist, or anyone for whom it is important to maintain that there are meanings and determinate translation, can make to Quine. The most direct is simply to insist that there really are analytic truths. For example, Grice and Strawson (1956) argued that there was a valid analytic-synthetic distinction even though it was not necessarily clear cut, and its validity could be demonstrated by an appeal to the difference in the methods by which sentences like:

(7) My 3-year-old child is an adult
(8) My 3-year-old child understands Russell's *Theory of Types*

could be verified. They claimed that of an infant prodigy it is just about conceivable that (8) could be verified, but however talented an infant was involved it is not clear what a sincere literal utterance of (7) would mean. However, Grice and Strawson concede that Quine is right about revisability, and so 'analytic' for them means 'analytic with respect to some conceptual scheme' (p. 430). In effect, therefore, they also concede Quine's major point, which is that necessary truths are necessary only with respect to some framework of beliefs.

Putnam (1962) while agreeing with Quine that many alleged examples of analytic truths, like 'cats are animals', are in fact revisable, argues nevertheless that there is a class of words which do generate analytic sentences. These are 'one-criterion' words, words in which all but one of a number of criteria associated with it can be occasionally ignored but for which this one criterion provides a necessary and sufficient condition for something falling under the term, and is used as such by a native speaker: that is, this criterion is part of the meaning of the word.

The problem with Putnam's suggestion is that it is extremely difficult to find examples which are wholly convincing. The example he gives himself:

(9) Someone is a bachelor if and only if he is an unmarried man

claims that divorcees, widowers and celibate priests are all bachelors, and it is not difficult to find people who do not share this intuition. Similar examples will usually provide scope for similar disagreements. Nevertheless, Putnam has certainly pointed to an important intuitive distinction: the relation between 'cat' and 'animal' seems to be 'less necessary' than that between 'bachelor' and 'unmarried'.

Katz (1975:85) also maintains that there are analytic truths and provides a criterion, in the context of the semantic theory elaborated in Katz (1972), for distinguishing between items that are semantically (i.e. analytically) associated with a word, and which should therefore be included in its dictionary entry, and those that are only contingently associated and so better described as a belief about its referent. The criterion is this:

> The answer to a question about whether a piece of information belongs in the dictionary entry for an item W is affirmative just in case there is some semantic property or relation whose extension in the language cannot be determined on the basis of the readings of the sentences in which W occurs unless these readings are projected compositionally from lexical readings for their morphemes in which the lexical reading for W contains semantic markers representing the information.

Unfortunately, as Katz tacitly concedes later (p. 86), this criterion is completely circular. It depends on being able to identify independently the 'semantic property' concerned – namely, in this case, analyticity. But this is supposed to be what the criterion was a criterion for. We are back where we started.

There are, then, two problems with this type of response. First, there is the problem of coming up with a sufficient number of clear examples to make the thesis that there are analytic sentences convincing. Many examples of supposedly analytic sentences ('cats are animals') turn out in fact to be revisable, and although 'bachelors are unmarried' may seem more secure this may just be an illusion. Certainly at a time when it is possible to rationally contemplate the possibility that even tautologies of the propositional calculus may be false, not just of some possible world, but of the actual world (Putnam, 1981:213), it would be as well to err on the side of caution.

Secondly, even if we grant that there is some substance to our intuition that some sentences just could not turn out to be false, we would still need to show that postulating meanings to explain this fact was not empty or circular. Quine objects that meanings too easily engender the illusion of having explained something if postulated uncritically. In any case, Quine thinks, he can explain our intuitions in terms of universally shared beliefs: we would need to show either that this explanation was unsatisfactory or that such beliefs were simply meanings by another name.

A second possible response is to attack the thesis of the indeterminacy of translation by arguing that Quine is unnecessarily and artificially restricting the data base that a translation manual is to be founded upon. His jungle linguist operates only with assent, dissent and 'bizarreness' reactions from his informants. This merely indicates Quine's behaviourist prejudices, it is argued, for the native speaker of a language has intuitions about entailment, semantic incompatibility and suchlike which go far beyond simple judgements of acceptability and unacceptability. Surely if this data was also to be accounted for the range of possible translation manuals compatible with the evidence would be severely reduced. Katz argues:

> (Quine's) ... claim about the existence of alternative non-synonymous translations might be thought easily refuted by the reply that such alternatives merely show the limitations of stimulus response theory and that a more sophisticated theory would provide us with a conception of linguistic evidence on which the translation of 'Gavagai'

as 'undetached rabbit part' would be a mistake. Perhaps such a conception would reveal the mistake in the form of higher confirmation for the opposite hypothesis that 'Gavagai' means 'Rabbit' (or in greater overall simplicity for the system containing the latter hypothesis ceteris paribus). The reply could spell out how the required linguistic evidence might be obtained in the following way. The field linguist might ask a bilingual native informant questions like 'Does "Gavagai" bear the semantic relation to "rabbit" that the first members of the following pairs (2.34) branch/tree, arm/body, roof/house, thumb/hand bear to the second members?' An affirmative answer by the native informant gives evidence for one of the hypotheses under consideration, and a negative answer gives evidence for the other. (1975:57-8)

The situation at this point becomes a little complicated. Quine himself (1972:449) would apparently resist this enrichment of the data base on the grounds that no operational account of concepts like synonymy or entailment can be given, and he would presumably also object to metalinguistic questions of the type Katz envisages. He seems therefore to invite Katz's (1975:58) rebuke that his claim about translation is sustained only by disqualifying the only possible evidence against it. However, as I understand him, Quine is being inconsistent here. Nothing in what he says denies that we, or the native speaker of our alien language, have intuitions of the (perhaps necessary) truth of examples like 'cats are animals', or 'red is a colour', merely that we do not need to invoke meanings to account for these intuitions. There seems to be some kind of suggestion that such judgements are already irredeemably tainted with a commitment to meanings in some way. But that is surely not so; such judgements are data − the basis for them is a matter for theory, whether the basis is meanings, as for Katz, or shared beliefs, as for Quine. So it would seem perfectly consistent and legitimate for a linguist to get assent to or dissent from sentences like 'If something is a cat, then it is an animal' and include these in his data.

Quine seems to be making the same mistake here as in his discussion of extensionally equivalent grammars (1972:448). There he poses the question: how do we decide which of two constituent analyses of a string ABC is correct, A-BC or AB-C? His 'unimaginative answer' is 'ask the natives'. But his discussion indicates that this question would be a translation of something like 'What is the correct constituent structure of ABC, please?' and he correctly points out that as most native speakers of English, including many who have studied linguistics, cannot readily answer such questions, we are making an unfair demand on our informant. But he then concludes from this that there is no right answer beyond simplicity or convenience. As Chomsky (1976:181) points out, this is simply not true. We can ask the natives: not directly, certainly, but by asking them whether, say, corresponding to *ABC and ADE* there is a paraphrase of the form *ABC and DE*. If there is, the criteria which we already use successfully for co-ordination in English and other languages would allow us to assign the structure A-BC to ABC. (Only constituents of an identical category can be conjoined.) We may not be logically sure that we are correct, but this is only inductive uncertainty, not indeterminacy.

It is exactly the same in making hypotheses about semantic structure: Quine's envisaged procedure using translations of technical terms like 'synonymous' is clearly absurd: 'what sort of semantic relation does "red" bear to "colour", please?' Just as clearly, we can elicit the judgements we want by using indirect and fairly cunning methods, but relying still on the same type of reaction as for observation sentences: assent, dissent or abstention. We are still asking the natives, but indirectly. I conclude that Quine's methodological objection is not valid, the proposed method being acceptable, even by his own rather stringent criteria.

Unfortunately, although we can justify some extension of the data base, the test suggested by Katz will cut no ice with Quine. Although, as we have seen, he could consistently allow judgements about intra-language relationships between sentences, Katz's test depends on inter-language judgements. And since the original hypothesis (which we assume Katz is accepting for the purposes of his argument) was that in terms of stimulus meaning, 'gavagai' and 'rabbit' were identical, the bilingual informant could only reply 'no' to Katz's question. He is being asked whether the semantic relation between 'gavagai' and 'rabbit' is the same as that between 'branch' and 'tree'. Since 'gavagai' and 'rabbit' are, by hypothesis, synonymous (in the only sense Quine can make of this) and 'branch' and 'tree' are not, he will always answer 'no', irrespective of the part/whole relationships involved.

As a matter of fact, even if we allow that the informant understands correctly what we are asking him to do, his reply of 'yes', which Katz would, I assume, take to indicate that 'undetached rabbit part' was the correct translation, would not remove the indeterminacy. For this is only one of the analytic hypotheses which would be consistent with this data: others might be that the semantic relation in question was 'belongs with', 'is joined to', 'is a typical feature of', etc. These are non-synonymous alternatives, but they each fit the data equally well. It appears, then, that even when the range of observations to be accounted for is extended, there is still room for indeterminacy.

IV

A third possible response, due to Chomsky, is to argue that translation is not indeterminate, but just under-determined. And that simply means that translation manuals are empirical theories: all theories which project beyond their founding data are under-determined, in physics just as much as in linguistics. We assume, as does the physicist, that there is 'a fact of the matter' even if our theories are only ever successively closer approximations to these facts. Quine, on the other hand, denies that for the linguist there is any such 'fact of the matter': linguistics and physics are in different boats in this respect:

> An actual field linguist would of course be sensible enough to equate 'gavagai' with 'rabbit', dismissing such perverse alternatives as 'undetached rabbit part' and 'rabbit stage' out of hand. This sensible choice and others like it would help in turn to determine his subsequent hypotheses as to what native locution should answer to the English apparatus of individuation, and thus everything would come out all right. The implicit maxim guiding his choice of 'rabbit', and similar choices for other native words, is that an enduring and relatively homogeneous object, moving as a whole against a contrasting background is a likely reference for a short expression. If he were to become conscious of this maxim, he might celebrate it as one of the linguistic universals, or traits of all languages, and he would have no trouble pointing out its psychological plausibility. *But he would be wrong; the maxim is his own imposition, towards settling what is objectively indeterminate.* It is a very sensible imposition and I would recommend no other. But I am making a philosophical point. (1971:146; my emphasis)

Chomsky's 'psychological realism' answer assumes that there is indeed a fact of the matter, and is based on observations about the process of learning a language, and on a parallel with the methodology of the theory of syntax. At the risk of retreading over-familiar territory we will spell out this parallel in some detail.

Quine's idealised account of the linguist doing radical translation — constructing a translation manual for an unknown language — can be seen in the same way as Chomsky's idealised account of the linguist's construction of a grammar, that is, as an abstract description of a child learning a first language. In this extremely radical idealisation the child is a clever scientist trying to construct a theory which will enable him to use the language he hears around him, just like Quine's jungle linguist. What sort of problems does he face?

There are many informal senses of 'theory' but one formal sense, the sense in which it is usually understood in linguistics: a theory consists of a set of proper or non-logical axioms stating its primitive concepts and their relations, and an inference mechanism of some kind: a standard logic. Let the set of observation sentences describing the data to be accounted for by such a theory be called D, and let these sentences be judgements of acceptability and unacceptability of certain strings of words mentioned in the sentences. A theory from which these observation sentences can be deduced will be said, in convenient shorthand, to entail the data (D) and will be said to be 'observationally adequate'. Now, let D be widened to include judgements of ambiguity, of sentence relatedness and so on; the kind of judgement which can be described by assigning to the string of words mentioned in each sentence a structural description. Call this D^*. Assume we have a theory T^1 such that T^1 entails D^*. Such a theory will be called 'descriptively adequate' and it will project beyond D^* in all interesting cases, for it will make claims about possible as well as actual sentences, and in this respect it can be said to represent the kind of knowledge which would be sufficient to make the judgements comprising D^*. (Sufficient only, not necessary.) Notice that although T^1 entails D^*, the reverse does not hold: D^* does not entail T^1. In other words the theory is not uniquely determined by the data. Thus if there is one theory, there will always be alternative theories $T^2 \ldots T^n$ such that they also entail D^*. Many of these would be only trivially different, but others might differ in a more substantial way and may not agree in their projections beyond D^* — they might make different claims about the range of possible sentences as yet unobserved, while agreeing over the observed sentences.

Chomsky makes the simplifying assumption that at best the child has access to D^*. But if the language learner only has access to D^* there is a problem in accounting for the fact that the kind of knowledge to be represented by T^1 — however it is actually represented — can be acquired at all. For since D^* does not entail T^1, or any of $T^2 \ldots T^n$, there could be no question of an inductive procedure at work leading automatically from data to theory. This means that whichever T a language learner arrives at, he must do so by a deductive process of hypothesis, testing, revision and amendment. Furthermore, since D* is finite, and does not entail T^1 there is always, as we have seen, more than one theory or set of hypotheses which is logically compatible with it. So, having granted that language learners must be able to make hypotheses about the T necessary to account for D*, the question now becomes one of how, among all the logically conceivable hypotheses which would be consistent with D*, he arrives at the 'right' one?

Chomsky argues that it is not the case that language learners have access to the full range of hypotheses logically compatible with D*. Rather they converge on a relatively narrow and constrained set of Ts. This is suggested by observation: the fact that the hypotheses selected agree in their projections beyond D* (even for different D*) — we all learn the same language. Furthermore, the hypotheses appear to be selected, according to Chomsky, in a rapid, uniform manner, and relatively independently of other cognitive and cultural influences. While we may not be absolutely sure that learners converge on exactly the 'same' T, it is clear that they converge on a range that appear to differ from each other only in small and apparently unimportant ways. Thus the answer to both problems, (how a T for D* can be arrived at in the first place, and why it is a T of that type and not some other T also entailing D*), is given by the claim that the range of conceivable hypotheses, or accessible Ts is much more highly constrained than just that set which entail D*. Only a small set of the logically possible hypotheses are ever considered.

Ts are of course, grammars, and the constraints on possible grammars are held, in this familiar story, to be the result of ultimately biological properties of the human brain. The relevant contrast is between the logically possible and the biologically or psychologically possible hypotheses.

The basis for choice between logically possible alternative theories of D* for the learner then, is psychological accessibility. For the linguist, this means that he must construct an explicit account of 'accessibility', of what makes one logical possibility a psychological possibility also. He must construct a metatheory (M) which will provide a motive for a choice between $T^1 \ldots T^n$, selecting that T (or those Ts) which are most favoured according to the principles of the metatheory we construct. Eventually, with the formulation of M, grammars of individual languages should be in large part predictable. M will supply the general principles which all and only grammars of human languages obey and only language-particular idiosyncrasies and lexical items will need to be added for a full description of the language. In this sense, M — the theory of universal grammar — will provide in a slightly limited sense an explanatory account of the grammar of the language, for it not only describes its 'shape', but also suggests why it is that shape and not some other conceivable shape which might do the job just as well.

Notice that, again, although M entails some subset of $T^1 \ldots T^n$, it is not itself entailed by that subset. M too is a hypothesis, then, about the conditions which would suffice (and may be necessary) for the formulation of some successful T on the basis of exposure to D^*. It is a hypothesis about the structural or functional properties of the mind, a hypothesis which in principle though not yet in practice is subject to refutation by neurophysiological investigation, since we assume that these structural-functional properties bear some relationships (though not necessarily revealing ones) to biological properties.

Returning to Quine, since, as we said, his field linguist can also be seen as an abstract description of a language learner, his situation can be represented in terms very similar to those above. The first language learner must construct a recursive system of rules and categories providing interpretations for the sentences of his language. We will assume that this theory meshes in with the grammar he is developing. He constructs a semantic theory or translation manual TM^1 of some domain D. For Quine, D consists of 'observation sentences': hypotheses about 'stimulus meanings', and TM^1 is a lexicon plus a system of analytic hypotheses. However, we have already seen that there is no reason not to expand D to D^*, including, as before, judgements of relations between sentences.

Again, since this theory, TM^1, entails D^* but not the other way round, and D^* is finite, there will always be other $TM^2 \ldots TM^n$ which also entail D^*. Quine's claim is this: all TMs are equally correct, provided they entail D. Preference for one TM over another — one system of analytic hypotheses over another — can only be based on a parochial, intuitive and unscientific feeling that one TM is somehow more 'natural' than another — a feeling for which, according to Quine, there is no rational warrant. Chomsky would argue that the analogy with syntax is to be taken seriously and pursued: observable facts about language learning, substantial agreement over interpretation between speakers, and fairly determinate translation between languages suggest that there is, as a matter of empirical fact, a convergence on a relatively narrow range of TMs.* And this, together with the fact that D^* does not entail

---

* A surprising consequence of Quine's claims is that I have no more right to assume that another speaker of English is operating with the same set of analytic hypotheses as I am, than I have to assume that of the speaker of a completely alien language.

any of the range of possible TMs, argues that learners must leap to hypotheses about the appropriate TM, and that the range of hypotheses accessible to the learner is relatively constrained by psychological, ultimately biological factors. If we do not assume this, the argument goes, it is difficult to see how any TM could be learned at all, let alone how such substantial uniformity of TMs could be arrived at. Pursuing further the analogy with syntax, the task for the linguist then becomes one of constructing a semantic metatheory (SM), which delimits the possible range of TMs and provides some principle for the selection of preferred alternatives in cases where there are several possibilities. SM in turn entails, though is not entailed by, some subset of $TM^1 \ldots TM^n$ and is also a hypothesis as to the structural functional properties of the mind, ultimately subject to neurophysiological evidence.

Given SM, the linguist can point to a basis for choice between various translation manuals, and so translation is not indeterminate, as Quine alleges, but merely under-determined, as is any hypothesis which goes beyond the data. 'Gavagai' would have to be translated as 'rabbit' since SM would rank the more exotic translations as, presumably, inaccessible to the first language learner. Such bizarre analytic hypotheses would not necessarily be beyond our conscious intellectual reach (and we might in future need them for translating Martian) but they would bear a similar relation to the preferred systems as the syntax of various artificial languages bears to the syntax of natural languages: they can be learned after a fashion, but as a game or intellectual exercise and not in the way in which we learn a first language.

The question of whether translation is indeterminate reduces then to the question of whether SM is an empirical theory. If it is, then there is something for it to be right and wrong about, namely whether or not there is a natural system of analytic hypotheses for humans, which we can therefore take as the 'right' one. If not, then translation is indeterminate.

An empirical theory is one which can be tested by examining the relevant 'fact of the matter'. Quine's standard for what counts as a 'fact' here is extremely rigid:

Quine has recast the matter in discussion by saying that his frame of reference for matters of fact is physical theory, that (analytic hypotheses) do not imply any truths of physics and in particular they have no implication for the state and distribution of elementary particles. (Hockney 1975:420)

Hockney goes on to point out that by the latter criterion it is likely that even some hypotheses of physics would not count as empirical for Quine, strictly speaking. However, even granting these rigid standards it is possible to argue that claims about analytic hypotheses are empirical. If there is some set of natural hypotheses for humans then this must be because of our constitution: we are built in such a way that we either have the hypotheses in question already at birth, or cannot help but develop them during the course of maturation (perhaps given also the nature of our interaction with the world we are born into). Even if the development of the analytic hypotheses is determined partly by social factors, it cannot be wholly determined by them. Either way, then, some features of our innate constitution must be involved. And unless some superstition about souls is invoked to explain this, our account will certainly have some implication (though perhaps not very directly) for the 'distribution of elementary particles', for our explanation of the properties in question will ultimately, we suppose, make reference to facts about human neurophysiology.[3]

Of course, this does not guarantee that any 'truths of physics' in the stronger sense of laws or generalisations of physics will be implied by this account. But as Hockney points out, if this requirement is meant literally, Quine must be endorsing a very strong brand of reductionism: that all facts of linguistics must reduce to, or be explained by, the laws of physics. It is not at all necessary to maintain such a strong thesis as this in order to claim that analytic hypotheses, and therefore SM, are empirical hypotheses: all that it requires is a commitment to materialism: to the claim that all psychological states (in the widest sense) can be given a physical description, in principle. This does not mean that this physical description will necessarily be very revealing, or that the laws of psychology or linguistics, if there are any, can be put into any correlation with the laws of physics, much less reduce to them. Most linguists are probably committed to a version of Davidson's (1974b) 'anomalous monism', which maintains that there are some facts of psychology which are not usefully reducible to facts of physics, but that this does not entail that there is a class of events over and above the class of physical events. Events may be described in either physical or psychological terms, and pairs of events may be related by laws under one description but not under the other. (See also J.A. Fodor 1975.)

So far then, we seem to be justified in assuming that SM can indeed be an empirical theory. In fact, at some points[4] Quine seems to agree with all of this and to be insisting merely that mental entities or psychological hypotheses should not receive their final justification only in terms of other mental entities. As a methodological prescription this is surely unobjectionable, even banal. At some point of course we want our linguistic hypotheses to link up with other parts of psychology and, eventually, to features of human biology, even though there may be no final reduction of them.

But other arguments have been put forward recently to the effect that Quine's indeterminacy thesis entails that even psychological theory, and hence linguistic theory, is itself indeterminate. Putnam (1978:42-5) argues that explanation, either scientific or everyday, is 'interest relative' in that what counts as a good explanation for some phenomenon is one which is consistent with a particular set of interests or 'explanation space'. An explanation may be logically adequate, in that the phenomena follow from the theory, but intuitively empty, if it does not fit in with the rest of our theories, or enable us to generalise the explanation to what we consider to be a relevant range of cases. There is no such thing as a good explanation *per se*. The indeterminacy of translation is just a special case of this interest-relativity, says Putnam. If Martians have different interests and preoccupations from us:

> the Martians might well find the most 'natural' translation of 'gavagai' to be the Martian expression that *we* translate as 'undetached rabbit part'. In short, 'indeterminacy of translation' (and reference) is plausible to *the extent* that it follows from the interest relativity of explanation. (p. 45)

It follows that psychological theories and the explanations provided by them can only ever be interest relative, and never 'objectively' correct. Putnam is willing to concede that there might be a correct 'functional' description of a person's linguistic abilities in the form, say, of an abstract computer program or 'machine table'. That is to say, there might be some theory which could in principle simulate aspects of someone's ability, for example, the ability to refer to objects by their name. But:

> this is quite different from supposing that there is an objectively correct description ... *in the sense of a psychological theory*, if by a psychological theory is meant a theory which employs notions like *interest, belief, desire,* etc. This is going to be my main point: indeterminacy of translation is equivalent to indeterminacy of the transition from functional organisation (in the sense of machine table, or whatever) *to* psychological description. (p. 49)

Whereas we might regard some subroutine of the program as corresponding to 'referring to a rabbit', a Martian might construe the same subroutine as corresponding to 'referring to a rabbit stage'. Therefore there is no 'objectively correct' psychological theory, and so no objectively correct SM.

Of course, Putnam is correct that for any theoretical hypothesis there will always be a potentially infinite number of coextensive alternative descriptions for which we may not be able to find any direct negative evidence ('This part of the machine table corresponds to referring to a rabbit and an invisible toad'). But as Chomsky argues, the same thing is true of physics or any other science: we can always dream up some bizarre alternative to a current hypothesis:

> We rely, in such cases, on concepts of simplicity, insight and explanatory power that are not at all understood and that are presumably rooted in our cognitive capacities. (1980:22)

To this extent, explanation *is* interest relative: we have some concept of a natural, or better, a useful explanation. If this is all there is to the indeterminacy of psychology then we have nothing very serious to worry about. What Putnam needs to show is not only that the alternative construal of the rabbit subroutine is not just a trivial alternative of the type just acknowledged, but also that on the other hand there is no 'fact of the matter' to enable us to determine whether our interpretation or the Martian's is the correct one. For if there is a fact of the matter, then psychological theories are not indeterminate.

Putnam cannot consistently do this, however. For Putnam agrees with Chomsky that there must be innately determined constraints on possible systems of analytic hypotheses; in order to account for the fact that human beings can in fact communicate with each other across different cultures, he says:

> There seems only one possible explanation: human *interests*, human *saliencies*, human cognitive processes, must have a *structure* which is heavily determined by innate or constitutional factors. (p. 56)

But then the claim that we are referring to rabbits and not rabbit stages is not indeterminate, for there must, if we are materialists, be a physical fact of the matter, difficult though it may be to get at revealingly. This being the case, if some functional theory can be interpreted in two different ways, as Putnam describes, then this simply shows that it is not detailed enough. If the functional description is a complete description, as he is assuming, then a subroutine for referring to rabbits will simply be different from a subroutine for referring to rabbit stages, even if from the 'outside' we cannot actually tell which subroutine is being executed on a particular occasion. Since there is a fact of the matter, Putnam must either maintain that for some reason we cannot in principle ever distinguish between two apparently coextensive descriptions, which is absurd, or admit the possibility of finding some such functional difference between the two subroutines.

V

There are, then, two different responses worth pursuing to the clutch of objections raised by Quine against the possibility of a theory of word meaning. One possibility would be to investigate further the claim that there are some analytic sentences. If there are, then learning the meaning of at least some words cannot be entirely a matter of acquiring beliefs about the world and so a theory of linguistic learning will not be wholly subsumed within a theory of non-linguistic learning. Furthermore, although the existence of analytic sentences in some language does not guarantee translation between languages, it does make it theoretically possible: if there is a something which can be expressed by a sentence – an idea, or proposition – independently of non-linguistic beliefs, then it is theoretically possible that a sentence of another language should express the same idea.

The other avenue is to explore the possibility of the formulation of a semantic metatheory as a response to the claim of indeterminacy of translation. If we can show that there is a motive for choice between rival translation manuals then we can show that translation is not indeterminate, merely underdetermined. This will involve us in an attempt to put some substance to the claim that what we are referring to by 'rabbit' is a whole, enduring physical object, rather than the manifestations of rabbithood, rabbitscapes or rabbit slices that our Martian friends may be referring to.

Notes

1. Quine's arguments can be found in various versions and in many places. The classic sources for discussion of the notions of meaning, the analytic and the synthetic, synonymy, etc. are 'Two Dogmas of Empiricism' and 'The Problem of

Meaning in Linguistics', both in Quine (1964) but reprinted elsewhere many times. The indeterminacy of translation is treated at length in *Word and Object* (1960); see also Quine (1971). The most recent extended discussion of language learning is in *The Roots of Reference* (1974).

2. Example (4) was true at the time of writing.

3. See also Hockney, p. 426.

4. Innate mechanisms '... may be yet more remotely theoretical, deep in the DNA; and I am just as receptive to such conjectures, regarding the mechanisms of language, as I am to the physicists' conjectures regarding elementary particles... In the extreme case where a theoretical element utterly devoid of observable manifestations is posited for the sake of some theroretical integration that it promises, I still say let us give it a try, recognising what we are doing. But let us scorn any purported justification of the posit in irreducibly mentalistic terms.' (Letter from Quine, quoted in Gibson 1980:367)

2 AGAINST SEMANTIC PRIMITIVES

I

The attempt to construct a semantic metatheory — a metatheory defining the notion 'possible semantic theory' or translation manual for a natural language — has proceeded for the most part in a way which has been exactly and deliberately analogous to the attempt to construct syntactic and phonological metatheories. (See, for example, Katz 1972: 32-4; Jackendoff 1976:89-91.) The aim has been to define a set of substantive and formal universals prescribing, in large part, the semantic theory for individual languages. As we have seen, the success of this enterprise would mean that Quine's indeterminacy claim could be denied by simply pointing to the semantic metatheory as a motive for choosing between alternative systems of analytic hypotheses, or alternative semantic theories, since this metatheory would define 'accessible' or 'natural' systems as would be required.

The distinction between formal and substantive universals is one of convenience and it is not absolute or given in nature. Still, it is possible to point to examples which fall fairly clearly in one domain or another: the assignment of coreference, scope of negation, interpretation of reciprocals and such like phenomena would be plausibly assumed to be subject to formal universals of some kind: probably constraints on the operation of rules of interpretation. Phonological features like '± voice', on the other hand, are assumed to be drawn from a set of substantive universals. Word meaning, and relations between non-logical words, for the most part have been similarly assumed to draw on substantive universals of many kinds. The dominant analogy here has in fact been with phonological theory, as the following quote will show:

> The very notion 'lexical entry' presupposes some sort of fixed, universal vocabulary in terms of which these objects are characterized, just as the notion 'phonetic representation' presupposes some sort of universal phonetic theory (Chomsky 1965:160)

For both Katz and Jackendoff (and all generative semanticists)[1] this universal vocabulary suffices for the description of word meanings, and the notion of word meaning itself, along with those semantic properties based on it are to be explicated by a partial or complete breakdown of the words into these smaller elements of meaning, elements of this universal vocabulary, which at least for Katz are directly relatable to the structure of the mind.

However, this analogy with the universal vocabulary of phonetics or phonology (which for the purposes of this argument we will take to be some system of distinctive features), cannot be continued when the question of its justification is raised. Distinctive features are, at least in principle, relatable to properties of the human vocal tract, to acoustic properties and properties of the human perceptual system. The range of possible distinctive features is constrained ultimately by human physiology. Thus, although they may be fairly abstract there are ways, with ingenuity, of arriving at a principled decision between alternatives, and most importantly, clear grounds for claiming that what is meant by, say, 'voicing' is the same in one language as in the next. Languages are strictly comparable in this respect because people's vocal tracts are also strictly comparable. However, there are grave difficulties facing any attempt to justify substantive semantic universals – semantic primitives – in any similar way. For since actual words or morphemes are language specific, it clearly cannot be these which are universal. If anything is universal then, it must be the concepts or meanings they express. This is what Katz and Jackendoff and by implication many practitioners of componential analysis claim. But the move from concrete words, where substantial agreement can in principle be obtained, to 'concepts' or 'meanings' is fraught with difficulty, for its legitimacy presupposes the very answer to Quine's objections that it is intended to provide. How do we know that 'the same concept' is expressed in different languages? Or even by different words in the same language?

Proponents of the 'semantic primitives' or 'sense components' approach have been willing to concede that the status of these entities is rather unclear. But it has apparently been assumed that this is a temporary lacuna to be filled in as work progresses. Katz, for example, identifies semantic markers with 'concepts' which are 'the objective content of thought processes' (1972:38) and maintains that:

> It is quite unreasonable to insist . . . that we provide a general definition of 'semantic marker' and 'reading' that clarifies the ontological status of the notions 'concept' and 'proposition'. (1972:39)

Jackendoff avoids discussion of this problem and adopts semantic markers as *pro tem* devices still representing concepts but without committing himself on the question of whether they are ultimate primitives or not (they are not, however, English words: 1976:91). The general situation is charitably described by J.D. Fodor: she says (referring specifically to claims about substantive rather than formal universals)

> the mentalism of much of the current linguistic research in semantics is not a working part of the theory but simply reflects the anti-behaviouristic conviction that there are ideas, that they do play a significant role in human activities and language use, and that when we eventually achieve an adequate theory of meaning, meanings and ideas will turn out to be closely interrelated. (1977:17)

From our point of view though, such charity is not an answer to Quine: if there are substantive universals in the shape of semantic primitives we should be able to point to them, or at least to their effects, and not merely fall back on pious hopes about what will emerge from a completed semantic theory.

II

Various critics have, from the earliest days, cast doubt on the existence of semantic primitives: Bolinger (1965), Lewis (1972:170), J.A. Fodor (1975), Kempson (1977:101-2), Lyons (1977:332-5) and Sampson (1979, 1980), though their use in semantic description continues to be widespread (see note 1). The problem is that it is very difficult to show conclusively that something does *not* exist. However, what we can do is to try to show that, whether they exist or not, the use of such entities is beset with insuperable methodological problems. The most telling line of argument concerns the individuation of these semantic atoms, and their relation to the symbols claimed to represent them.

If, as Katz stresses, it is true that:

> although the semantic markers are given in the orthography of a natural language, they cannot be identified with the words or expressions of the language used to provide them with suggestive labels (1972:299)

then any set of symbols providing an identical range of different 'words' would suffice to represent the primitives of which (real) words consist. The relationship between these symbols and the concepts they express should be no more or less difficult to state than the relationship between what look like English words '(Human) (Male)', (but aren't) and the same concepts (see Lewis 1972:170; Lyons 1977:332-5). But of course once such a substitution is made it becomes much less obvious that the analysis of words in terms of semantic markers is in any way 'giving a meaning': the representation of 'bachelor' as

(1) (214B) (25C) (PQR) ...

rather than

(2) (Physical Object) (Living) (Human) (Male) (Adult) (Never married)

is theoretically unobjectionable on Katz's own admission, for the contents of the brackets in (2) are not, despite appearances, English words any more than the contents of the brackets in (1) are. However, the systematic substitution of suitable figures and signs (according to the semantic metatheory) makes it perfectly clear that what is being done here pending further elaboration is a translation of honest English words into some obscure code. Until an explanation of the code is given we might as well, as Lewis remarks, be translating into Latin.

Katz's response to this is to press an analogy between chemical descriptions such as

$$(3) \quad \begin{matrix} & H & \\ H : & \ddot{C} & : H \\ & H & \end{matrix}$$

and semantic markers (which have a syntactic structure in more complex examples). He says that in order to understand (3),

> we have to know the relevant portions of chemical theory: we have to understand that configurations of symbols like [our 3] represent electronic structures, that the element designations represent the kernel of atoms consisting of a nucleus and inner electrons, and that the dots represent paired electrons in the valence shell held jointly by two atoms. Likewise, to know what a reading claims about the semantic structure of a sentence, we have to know the relevant portion of semantic theory: we have to understand that certain semantic markers designate certain concepts and that the formal relations among the symbols in a semantic marker represent certain

specific relations among the components of the concept designated by the marker. (1975:109)

This is exactly the right answer for someone in Katz's position to give. If semantic markers are theoretical entities, then what is being claimed by his approach to semantic description is not that what someone knows when they understand a sentence is that the sentence maps onto a set of symbols, but that it maps onto the concepts represented by those symbols. Lewis's objection that translation into Markerese tells us nothing about the relationship between the sentence and the conditions under which it would be true would presumably not hold if the metatheoretical explanation which Katz mentions was available, for a grasp of the concept as thus explicated would provide a grasp of exactly this relationship.

Unfortunately, Katz's attempted response fails, not in principle but in practice, for it makes appeal to a non-existent portion of 'semantic theory'. When we look to find some account of the relationship between semantic markers and the concepts which he claims they designate, we find nothing of any substance at all, merely the reiterated conviction that such concepts do exist; that they are universal; that they are a result of innate properties of the brain; and that they are designated by elements which, for convenience only, look like English words. The analogy with chemistry fails for the same reason that the analogy with phonology which we mentioned earlier also fails: whereas a chemist can point to samples of hydrogen and carbon, and (indirectly) to the configurations of electrons resulting in the formation of compounds, Katz cannot point to the concept (Human) or (Male) nor to the means whereby these atoms are alleged to form compounds. Nor can he point to the extension of these concepts (assuming that concepts are the kind of thing that have extensions) for then he has to answer Quine's original question: how can you be sure that it is *that* particular concept of which this is the extension, rather than some different coextensive one?

The failure of the attempt to construct semantic theory and semantic components along lines analogous to syntactic and phonological theory becomes apparent when we consider a development of Lewis's objections (see the introduction to Evans and McDowell 1976). Syntactic, phonological and semantic components alike are supposed to describe the competence of a native speaker, his tacit knowledge of the language on which he draws in performance. A reasonable requirement on the intelligibility of appeals to tacit knowledge and competence is that description of this knowledge should be such that an explicit knowledge of the description should be sufficient (not necessary, of course) for the exercise of the competence being described.[2] (In the case of syntactic competence, the question of quite how we would tell that this competence is being exercised is a difficult one, given the many interacting cognitive systems involved in actual performance. I shall sidestep this problem, as before, by assuming that we are only dealing with grammars that do not interact in any significant way with other systems. This idealisation is most unlikely to be true, but that is not important for the argument.)

Consider now a person of prodigious memory and awe-inspiring ability in the manipulation of axiomatic systems, who has committed to memory a fully explicit syntax and lexicon for some language previously unknown to him, say Hopi. Let us also assume that there is a parsing algorithm for this grammar which he has also committed to memory. Such a superman would be readily agreed to have an explicit knowledge of the grammar of Hopi. Furthermore, we can make sense of the claim that what he knows corresponds to the implicit knowledge we attribute to the native speaker of Hopi (as far as syntax is concerned) because on exposure to a string of Hopi morphemes, our prodigy can say whether that string is grammatical or ambiguous by running through the parsing algorithm to see whether it terminates with one, two or no parses (in the case where the string is ungrammatical). He can duplicate the ability of the native speaker in this respect.

It seems to be likewise in phonology: our prodigy could memorise the phonological component of a grammar of Hopi, and provided we are prepared to credit him with knowledge of phonological metatheory, he would be able to say, of any well-formed string of Hopi morphemes, how they were to be pronounced. His explicit knowledge of a phonological description of Hopi is not a mere mechanical pairing of sets of complex symbols at the systematic phonemic level with a partially overlapping set of symbols at the systematic phonetic level, because he knows from the metatheory what the value of these symbols is. He knows that they represent certain articulatory gestures and configurations. Again, explicit knowledge would be sufficient for competence.

In the case of a semantic theory, things are different. Someone with an explicit knowledge of a Katz or Jackendoff type semantic theory could associate with every well-formed string of morphemes one or more structures containing semantic atoms of some kind. In the case of semantics the competence being described is the understanding of a sentence. Does explicit knowledge of a semantic component of Hopi suffice for this? Clearly not: what is needed, as Katz points out, is also a grasp of the terms of semantic metatheory (atoms, projection rules, etc.) employed in a semantic component. But as we have already stressed, unlike the primitives of syntax and phonology, no metatheoretical account exists of the primitive concepts referred to. Unfortunately, in the absence of such an account, the explicit grasp of a semantic component suffices merely to provide the ability to pair symbols from one vocabulary (Hopi) with those of another (semantic metatheory). Obviously, something more than this is required to understand a language. The supposed parallel with syntax and phonology breaks down.

III

Of course, the fact that Katz has not offered an explanation of the metatheoretical relationship between markers and concepts does not necessarily mean that it is not possible to give one. Ultimately, I do not think that it is possible, but there have been several interesting attempts in this direction. For example, the analogy which Katz draws between chemical elements and semantic primes is pursued in an interesting article by Zwicky (1973) which is to my knowledge the only place in which explicit criteria for semantic atoms are offered. He describes a 'substance theory of semantic primes', which he offers as an 'organising hypothesis'. Organising hypotheses are 'high level assumptions, fundamental empirical hypotheses'. Furthermore:

> they are not easily given up, even in the face of apparent counter-examples, which will be treated as manifestations of minor complicating principles or as outright anomalies (see Kuhn 1962). It is this resistance to disproof that gives organising hypotheses their field-defining nature. They are testable, in some sense, and they can be abandoned after argument, but the tests are not simple nor the arguments straightforward. (p. 471)

The Substance Theory hypothesises that:

> every semantic prime is realisable as a lexical unit (root, inflection, or derivational affix) in some natural language. (p. 473)

This is, he says, analogous to the requirement that chemical elements be isolable substances: a rather primitive requirement reflecting the undeveloped state of semantic theory.

Zwicky's theory is an attempt to equate semantic primes with the 'basic' elements occurring in languages. As the theory is framed it is in fact far too liberal. Someone who postulated *CATHEDRAL* as a semantic prime could point for justification to the fact that it is 'realised' as 'cathedral' ('cathédrale', etc.). But Zwicky's remarks elsewhere suggest that he intends it to be restricted in the obvious way, to meaningful 'grammatical' elements of a language and to that part of the lexical vocabulary which is in some sense basic. As he remarks, in practice this is exactly what all previous investigators have done. But does the elevation of this practice into an organising principle make it any more empirical? Zwicky points out that the crucial word in the framing of a substance theory is 'realisable'. He says:

> English *and*, in one of its senses, realizes the prime AND because, aside from any syntactic or stylistic peculiarities associated with this sense of English *and*, its properties are those of an entity which bears certain specific relations to other entities (for example, OR, NOT, IF, ONE) which, taken together, form the basis for a semantic description of English. Among the relations in question is the duality of AND and OR — that AND is equivalent to NOT — OR — NOT and, conversely, that OR is equivalent to NOT — AND — NOT, or, stated precisely, that R AND S is equivalent to NOT ((NOT R) OR (NOT S)) and that R OR S is equivalent to NOT ((NOT R) AND (NOT S)). Just as one sense of *and* corresponds to AND, so one sense of *similar* corresponds to (realizes) LIKE, *become* and *-en* correspond to INCHOATIVE, and *say* corresponds to ASSERT. (p. 475)

Here Zwicky seems to be saying that we are justified in sometimes associating the AND of first order logic with the 'and' (as a sentential conjunction) of English, because, in connection with OR, NOT, IF, THEN, we have an explicit account of the nature of some of the inferences which native speakers of English are able to make with 'and', 'or', 'not' and 'if-then'. This is perfectly correct: we are justified in associating 'and' with AND precisely because we have an explicit semantic account of the latter (in the form of truth tables, for example) — we can define it just about as rigorously as anything can be defined. But the extension of this procedure which is made by Zwicky, to the claim that one sense of 'similar' corresponds to LIKE, and of 'become' and '-en'[3] to INCHOATIVE is not valid. It is not valid because there exists no analogous semantic treatment of elements like LIKE and INCHOATIVE — indeed, it seems likely that 'casual enrichment' of most systems of logic with such elements would preclude any satisfactory semantic account in the usual terms of a recursive definition of truth for the sentences in which they appear (see the introduction to Evans and McDowell 1976).[4] What we need in order to justify the putative realisation of primes as particular lexical units is some kind of assurance that 'similar' (sometimes) means LIKE which does not depend on the fact that as English speakers we recognise that LIKE is 'like' in capital letters. In order to ensure that no such dependence exists we should substitute for LIKE, as before, some arbitrary sign, say B 25, and again as before, it is immediately much less obvious that any progress has been made, for we have no idea what B 25 means. A similar treatment of AND, however, is quite possible: a semantic theory which associated *and* with X14, and defined X14 as having the properties that S_1-X14-S_2 is true if and only if S_1 and S_2 are true, that from S_1-X14-S_2 we can infer S_1, or S_2 and so on, would fulfil most of the basic requirements of adequate semantic descriptions. I conclude that the attempt to specify 'realisability' in these terms meets the same problems as previous attempts to account for relations between primes and words.

There is an alternative way of construing Zwicky's proposals (though it is one for which there is little or no warrant in his article) along the following lines. If we pursue this alternative, we are led to some interesting and not altogether obvious conclusions about the relationship between 'conceptual breakdown' and truth theories. Consider the claim that AND, LIKE and INCHOATIVE are semantic primes in the sense that they are part of a basic sub-vocabulary of English (and distinguished from the rest of English only by being in capital letters) suitable for the partial or total description of many other English words which they can, in combination, paraphrase. There is no pretence that they are anything other than English words in fancy dress; LIKE is not realised as 'similar', but as 'like', and the enterprise of semantic description on the level of word meaning is the adoption of this sub-vocabulary as a metalanguage, in a way which is no different from, though hopefully more accurate and revealing than the practice of lexicographers in giving a paraphrase of complex words in terms of combinations of less complex words. Thus to analyse a word like 'kill' as CAUSE TO BECOME NOT ALIVE, or 'frighten' in its transitive sense as CAUSE TO BECOME AFRAID, is to assert a correspondence, not between an English word and a series of concepts represented by symbols (coincidentally looking like English words), but between a complex English word and a structure containing less complex English words.

In time, perhaps, we might also feel justified (given some co-operative bilinguals) in asserting partial correspondences (translations) between 'basic' English and 'basic' French, Swahili or Urdu. We might then feel justified in asserting that 'cause' in English represents the same concept as various roots and morphemes in other languages and claiming it, and other such examples, as substantive semantic universals. We would feel justified in making these assertions because LIKE, CAUSE and so on, would be part of a semantic metalanguage which was being used (as opposed to mentioned) by us as investigators, in the same way that the rest of English is used by us. Then we can feel confident that 'kill' means 'cause to become not alive' (if it does) because we are making intuitive judgements about the only thing in linguistics which we can make intuitive judgements about: the status of sentences and relationships between words, phrases and sentences of our native language.

In the absence of a satisfactory account of the relationship between semantic primes and the concepts they are supposed to represent, such an approach as this, if we are determined to reduce words to primitives at all, is the only coherent and empirical one. It amounts to a much more severe version of Zwicky's Substance principle, one which demands that the basic elements of semantic description should *be* (simple) roots, inflections or derivational affixes, not merely that the elements should be 'realisable' as these, for this involves us in the same dilemma which we started out by trying to avoid.

Adopting this view of the nature of semantic description — that it should be part of an existing language in use — has the interesting consequence that if we aim for reasonable standards of rigour we are now forced to the conclusion that something like a theory of truth for a language is the correct way of accounting for its compositional nature — in so far as this includes those combinatory elements relevant for logical inference — and that in so far as a Katz type semantic theory amended along the lines just suggested attempts to capture similar insights, it is a notational variant of such an approach. This can be seen by what is essentially a reverse of Davidson's (1967b) argument that a theory of truth meeting Tarski's *convention T* is a semantic theory for a natural language.

A truth theory of the type Davidson has in mind is supposed to provide, for each well-formed sentence of a natural language, a description of its truth conditions: a 'T-sentence'. T-sentences are deducible from the T-theory, where this is a finitely stated recursive mechanism giving a truth- and inference-relevant structural description for each sentence of the object language and a description of its truth conditions in the metalanguage, and correct pairings of these two over an infinite range of sentences. (In fact, many other requirements are apparently needed to ensure complete adequacy as a theory of meaning: see Evans and McDowell (1976); Platts (1979). These refinements are not directly relevant here.) The triviality of

(4) 'Snow is white' is true if and only if snow is white

is only apparent, for (4) results from a theory which also provides T-sentences like:[5]

(5) 'John swore violently' is true in the mouth of Speaker S at time T and place P if and only if there is some event e such that e is a swearing, and e is by John and e is violent and e is at some t^i, t^i before T.

Or, in an obvious notation:

(6) 'John swore violently' true$_{S,T,P}$ ↔
    $[(\exists e) (\text{Swearing}(e) \wedge \text{By}(\text{John}, e) \wedge \text{Violent}(e))]_{ti}$, $ti < T$

The construction of a theory issuing mechanically in such T-sentences for each sentence of the object language is not a trivial enterprise. T-sentences are saved from triviality in another way too: the metalanguage in which the truth definitions are framed is either a form of English, a regimented sublanguage of English, or an artificial language for which there exists an explicit semantics (first order predicate calculus) or a combination of both. Thus the semantic theorist can be sure that his definitions, his T-sentences, really do give the truth conditions for the object language sentences (that the right-hand side of them really does capture what the left-hand side means): the metalanguage is being used, not mentioned (there are quotation marks only around the object language sentence). This state of affairs is to be contrasted with what has previously been pointed out about Markerese semantics. Here we have a finitely stated, recursive theory issuing in, say, M-sentences, for every well-formed object language sentence, of the form:

(7) 'John is a bachelor' has a semantic representation (or means that) 'John is (PHYSICAL OBJECT) (LIVING) (HUMAN) (MALE) (ADULT) (NEVER MARRIED) . . . '

The objection which we quoted earlier was on the grounds that since both object language and metalanguage sentences are quoted, all that is being done here is to pair one set of symbols with another. The only way to break out of this circle would be to use the metalanguage expressions. However, this we cannot easily do: it is not just a matter of erasing a pair of quotes. Markerese is not a natural language – in particular it is not English, according to Katz. But since there is no explicit account given elsewhere of the semantics of Markerese, of how Markerese operates (sanctions certain inferences, disallows others, etc.) unlike the case of the predicate calculus for example, we can never be sure, as semantic theorists, that our M-sentences state what they ought to state: the meaning of the object language sentences mentioned in them. Within a T-theory, though, we can be sure that our T-sentences state truth conditions, for we are using familiar words and syntax.

The way to really break out of the circle is to bring out into the open what has always been obvious but unadmitted: that Markerese is English in capital letters, and furthermore to recognise that this is not necessarily circular or trivial. For now we can be sure, as semantic theorists, that our M-sentence, amended as in

(8) 'John is a bachelor' means that John is a physical object, living, human, male, adult and has never married.

really does state the meaning of the object language sentence (if it does). We might also want to avail ourselves of a convenient formalism, and an account of the inferential capabilities implicit in such conjoinings of predicates, thus:

(9) 'John is a bachelor' means that Physical Object (John) $\wedge$ Living (John) $\wedge$ Human (John) ... etc.

Clearly, the construction of a theory resulting in sentences like (9) for every well-formed sentence of English is as non-trivial an enterprise as the construction of a truth theory issuing in sentences like (6). It is, in fact, exactly the same enterprise: for if we now substituted everywhere for 'means that' the phrase 'is true if and only if' the result would be an extensionally equivalent theory. This was exactly the point of Davidson's original arguments in favour of a Tarski type T-theory: in place of the obscure 'means that' we could substitute the (allegedly) better understood 'true if and only if' and the result, given certain plausible assumptions, would be extensionally indistinguishable from it as regards its output. A truth theory would give us everything we could require from a theory of meaning, namely it would tell us, for every sentence of the language, the conditions under which it would be true. Thus it would be an acceptable substitute for a theory of meaning.

The reason why descriptions like (8) appear to be more revealing than those like (4) is because they incorporate some of the work a dictionary would do in its entry for 'bachelor'. If we omitted all mention of such relationships between words, or in Davidson's own words, adopt a theory that 'leaves the whole matter of what individual words mean exactly where it was' (1967:15) then we are still left with a perfectly respectable edifice: an account of the contribution of individual logical-grammatical structures (articles, quantifiers, conditionals, negation, modals, etc.) to the truth conditions of the sentences in which they appear, and an account of their possibilities of combination. But that is all: once we know the logical form of, for example:

(10) X is a good Y

then what a truth theory has to tell us about particular substitutions from the English lexicon for X and Y is entirely trivial. Thus the only advantage that a Markerese style theory, amended along the lines above, would have over an ordinary truth theory, would depend on the adequacy of the dictionary definitions it provided, now construed as being given in terms of some subset of English.

IV

If we make the decision to identify primitive semantic elements with some subclass of English words, abandoning for the time being attempts at universality, we confront a problem which those who equate semantic primes with abstract concepts have been able to dodge consistently. For, once we can bring the full range of our intuitions as native speakers to bear on the question of whether atomic reductions of words are adequate or not, we are forced to the conclusion that in the vast majority of cases such reductions are inadequate as full specifications of meaning. I am assuming that a full specification of the meaning of a term will be in the form of a biconditional, with the term entailing and entailed by its definition. That is to say, a satisfactory definition of a term will provide necessary and sufficient conditions for its application. Clearly, we are now back to the question of whether or not there are any analytic sentences, for if we have a definition meeting these conditions then the statement of that definition will be a sentence which is true by virtue of its meaning: namely, an analytic sentence.

We saw earlier that Putnam's example of 'bachelor' was not uncontroversial; similar examples of proposed definitions likewise generate controversy (see the literature on 'kill' as 'cause to die' as a representative instance: McCawley 1968a,b; J.A. Fodor 1970: Chomsky 1971; Lakoff 1972). This difficulty in finding satisfactory definitions is, unfortunately for us, exactly what would be predicted by Quine's account of the status of meanings. And at first sight, it looks as if things go Quine's way here, for it is not possible to argue that this apparent failure to come up with adequate and uncontroversial definitional equivalences is merely a matter of some imperfection on the part of linguists, or some temporary manifestation of the primitive nature of our knowledge. It is surely not a wholly contingent matter that even the most careful work seems to be inadequate in this respect. For example, the detailed and systematic attempt by Wierzbicka (1972) to describe parts of English according to the method outlined above (i.e. treating primitives as a sublanguage of English), while interesting and ingenious, produces analyses which fail the most basic test of synonymy — that one side of the equivalence must be true if the other is. Take this example:

(11) X feels afraid = X feels as one does when one thinks that something bad can happen to one which one cannot cause not to happen and which one diswants (= doesn't want) to happen.

Now, undoubtedly many situations describable by the right-hand side could also be described by the left-hand side. But equally, many could not: imagine someone contemplating the decimating of his salary by the Inland Revenue, an event which he cannot forestall, and being convinced that his industry should be fully rewarded, is considered something bad, and which he does not want to happen. Since this person is thinking that something bad can happen to him which he cannot cause not to happen and which he diswants to happen, he is presumably also feeling as one does when one thinks that. But he is not necessarily feeling afraid — more likely angry, or frustrated, or even resigned. It seems clear that what has been done here is to state an entailment from the left-hand side to the right-hand side: but the reverse entailment does not hold, and so this statement is not a full rendering of the meaning of 'feel afraid'.

If we re-interpret Katz's semantic markers as basic English, and do not allow the mysterious relation between symbols in brackets and concepts to suspend our disbelief, it becomes apparent that many of his definitions or 'readings' are inadequate. He says:

> The reading of the most familiar sense of 'chase' is represented: (((Activity ((Physical) ((Movement) ((Speed) (Fast) (Following Y)) ((Purpose) ((To catch Y)))))). (1972:101)

Disregarding the internal syntactic structure of this example, Katz's gloss makes it clear that the first three markers describe 'chase' as an action verb of physical motion, the marker (Speed) distinguishes it from words like 'creep' and (Following Y) distinguishes it from verbs like 'wander'. Katz also says that:

> it is necessary that the person or group doing the chasing have the purpose of trying to catch the thing being chased, which is indicated by the semantic marker '(Purpose)' together with the semantic marker it encompasses. (p. 102)

This groups 'chase' with 'pursue'. But is what Katz says about the meaning of 'chase' true? He certainly needs a marker to distinguish 'chase' from verbs like 'follow' and 'trail'. And it is certainly true that you can 'chase' someone and not 'catch' them, as Katz notes:

(12) He chased him but did not catch him

is not contradictory. But surely I can also chase someone without even intending to catch them?

(13) He chased him, intending only to frighten him away.

(13) is not contradictory, although it looks as if it ought to be on Katz's analysis. Katz would apparently account for this by pointing to the fact that he is using the marker (Purpose) rather than (Intention), saying

> activities have purposes but not intentions. It is left open to what extent the persons engaged in an activity having a fixed purpose themselves have the associated intention. (pp. 102-3)

This seems to imply that the verb 'chase' applies to an activity which has the purpose described, but that in some cases people who are chasing may not have the intention of achieving this purpose. But if that was the case, then the *activity* that such people are engaged in cannot be said to have that purpose (unless they are unaware of what they are doing) and so, if Katz's 'reading' is to be taken seriously, could not truly be described as 'chasing'. We have a dilemma: if we abandon the (Purpose) marker, then the reading of 'chase' is identical to that of several other verbs, since it is an activity lacking the required purpose. This makes false claims of synonymy, but if we retain the marker we also make false claims about the use of 'chase' in English. If we choose the former course we might consider using 'distinguishers' as understood in Fodor and Katz (1964) to provide the necessary distinction, but since in Katz's later work distinguishers play a reduced role, marking 'purely perceptual distinctions' (1972:84) it seems unlikely that they would be adequate here. The conclusion to be drawn from this is that where they are accurate, Katz's readings express entailments from the term under analysis, but that they do not constitute a biconditional definition, or full analysis of the meaning of that term.

It would be tedious to examine long lists of such examples. The general point is this: since our semantic primitives are English words, a metalanguage in use, we can no longer leave the explanation of the residue of meaning which seems to remain after these supposedly complete analyses to some forthcoming account of the relation between semantic primes and concepts. We are not able, for example, to claim as Lakoff does (1971:272) that the meaning of the prime is 'included' in that of the words. It is only the pretence that English words in parentheses or capitals are not English words that allows us to suspend our disbelief about the accuracy of the analyses.

If we turn our attention away from these theoretical definitions and search instead for pre-existing synonymies we do not seem to fare any better. Such pre-existing synonymies would provide us with an answer to Quine. If we could provide some criterion of synonymy between individual words, and show that by this criterion there were synonymous pairs of words then even though this would probably not count as a revealing analysis of the meaning of either of the words in question we would have satisfied Quine's criterion for demonstrating the existence of some entity ('no entity without identity'). We would have provided conditions for identity or sameness of meaning and showed that something met those conditions.

Unfortunately, it is easy to show that potential candidates for synonymous words (more accurately, lexical items) evoke the same response as attempts at definition. It is nearly always possible to find cases where we would be happy to use one but not the other. Binnick (1972) provides many such situations for good prima facie candidates like 'will' and 'be going to', other plausible candidates like 'begin' and 'start', or 'finish' and 'end' are similar:

(14) a The concert began
     b The concert started
     c ? the engine began
     d the engine started

(15) a The concert finished
     b The concert ended
     c The petrol finished
     d ? The petrol ended

Many people will argue that we are simply using too strict a criterion of synonymy. But this objection does not help us. There is surely a perfectly clear criterion of word and phrase synonymy, namely, metalinguistic and opaque contexts apart, that they are interchangeable in all contexts. This (apart from the reference to metalinguistic and opaque contexts) is pre-theoretic in that it makes no appeal to anything other than native intuitions. The criterion is perfectly straightforward, able to be met in principle, and probably is met by explicitly defined terms; it is just that by this criterion, there are very few other, if any, synonymous pairs of items. No doubt other criteria can be found which will make for more synonymy but these will either invoke theoretical distinctions which are just as problematic as analyticity and synonymy, like 'true and appropriate' vs. 'technically true though inappropriate', or some other distinction which presupposes an operational definition of synonymy; or be faced with the problem of accounting for the fact that allegedly synonymous expressions cannot be interchanged everywhere.

V

Quine would see, then, in the failure of our attempt to find satisfactory examples of definitions,[6] or of pre-existing synonymies, considerable support for his contention that there are no such things as meanings associated with words, where meanings are conceived of as belief-independent and determinate — though abstract — entities. For it seems that the usual response of people to alleged instances of synonymy is to try to imagine circumstances in which they would be prepared to apply one of the relevant terms and not the other — unmarried men who aren't bachelors, and so on. The Quinean suggestion would be that the picture which best fits this kind of observation is not one of comparing sense components for identity, a process which should surely yield a quick and definite answer, but rather one of a testing of associated beliefs, and consequences of those beliefs, to see how much overlap and discrepancy is possible, and how much individual beliefs can be changed. The greater the overlap, and the fewer beliefs that are able to be changed, the more we are inclined to judge pairs as synonymous.

This claim has some plausibility, for as Quine and Davidson have often remarked, questions such as whether two expressions are synonymous ought, if meanings are entities, to be quite sharp and clear cut, just as the question of whether two chemical compounds contain the same elements in the same proportions is clear cut. That is, they should have clear identity criteria. But in fact the contrast between judgements of identity of meanings and identity of other linguistic properties is striking: there is no difficulty in judging two pronunciations of the same sentence as identical, no difficulty in judging two utterances which are phonetically different as being utterances nevertheless of the same sentence type, not even much difficulty in deciding whether two sentences have the same syntactic structure, depending on the level of abstractness of this structure. Judgements of grammaticality can be difficult, but we have a welter of clear cases. But judgements of meaning of the type under discussion seem to have a different status altogether: even the 'clear cases', on inspection, are not so clear.

A possible comeback for the dedicated devotee of meanings would be to construct an explanation for the instability of our synonymy judgements along these lines: the pairs of expressions encountered above are synonymous on a technical definition of synonymy (to be elaborated and made specific somewhere or other) but people's intuitions about them are subject to interference from a different phenomenon possibly to be described in the theory of communication. For example, Searle (1975) notes that 'be able to', unlike 'can', cannot be used to convey an indirect request.

(16) Are you able to open the door?

can usually only be construed as a sarcastic request when understood non-literally. Searle's suggestion is that when a non-idiomatic or roundabout expression of a meaning is chosen rather than its idiomatic or direct expression this carries an extra pragmatic implication specific to the context. We could extend this to other cases of supposed synonymy. Thus if someone said 'John is a man who has never married', this would be taken to be implying something over and above what would be usually implied by using 'bachelor': perhaps that John does not match the usual connotations of 'bachelor'. The claim would be that although these are two different ways of saying the same thing, the choice of one way of saying it over another itself carries some semantic or pragmatic load, and that this is generally the case for such examples, urging us always to envisage something which could account for this difference. Hence we will always, as co-operative conversationalists, work hard to find some distinction.

This is an attractive view, and it may well be that a successful explanation along these lines will be forthcoming. However, there is a much simpler response to Quine. We can concede that supposed examples of analytic definitions are only conditional, for the most part, not biconditional. We can even concede that there are no true examples of synonymy to be found (though we might want to be cautious and reserve judgement on this question). The response is simply to point out that neither of these things is incompatible with the existence of some genuine analytic relations between words. For if we are looking for some clear-cut semantic judgements we can point to the striking fact that judgements of entailment are far more secure than judgements of synonymy. I may not be sure whether 'bachelor' is fully synonymous with 'unmarried man', but I am sure that if someone is truly describable as a bachelor then he is also truly describable as an unmarried man. If I know what 'chase' means, then I know that it entails that some physical action is being carried out which involves following something at a relatively fast speed. But not every physical action involving following something at a relatively fast speed is an act of chasing.

To claim that there are some analytic relations between words is of course quite compatible with the non-existence of true lexical synonymy (though it does make it a theoretical possibility). A well-known example of a sub-vocabulary which is structured in such a way is the domain of colour words. There seem to be many secure entailments ('If this is scarlet, then it is red'), but it is as difficult there as elsewhere to find clear and uncontroversial synonyms.

We can also concede to Quine that many examples which have appeared to be analytic might turn out to be revisable, and that to some extent he is correct that many words have their meaning by virtue of their place in a network of beliefs about the world, rather than having 'meanings' as traditionally conceived attached invisibly to them. In fact, if the only secure semantic judgements we can make have the form of a conditional, we can accept that it is true of *all* words that they do not have meanings as traditionally conceived attached to them. For conditionals of the type illustrated do not give a full specification of the meaning of the term: they provide only necessary conditions, not conditions which are both necessary and sufficient. Thus they do not correspond to the traditional conception of a meaning (and we can in any case accept that the uncritical postulation of such entities seems to be a methodological dead end).

Nevertheless, after all these concessions, we can insist that even if these conditionals only give a partial specification of the meaning of the term, it is still true that the connection between the words in the antecedent and the words in the consequent is a semantic and not a contingent connection. We may discover that cats are or are not animals, but we do not discover as a fact about the world that bachelors are unmarried, or that circles are round. Quine's attempt to explain these judgements in terms of shared non-linguistic beliefs is either inadequate, or is an embracing of semantic connections under another name. If the beliefs connecting 'bachelor' and 'unmarried' are the same type of beliefs as those about Jones the butcher or about membership of the EEC then something quite fundamental about the firmness of such beliefs is missed out. For it is surely true that these beliefs *are* absolutely firm. Although as we have stressed throughout, caution is necessary over many examples of analytic sentences, these beliefs *are* unrevisable. It might be rational (though difficult) to contemplate giving up some tautologies of the propositional calculus for the sake of a consistent scientific explanation of quantum mechanics, but even the most adventurous thought-experimenter could not conceive of bachelors who were married, or circles that displayed not a trace of roundness. The propositional calculus is not part of our language, but of our theories; we do not, as native English speakers, have any sound intuitions about its tautologies. But a belief about the connection between 'bachelor' and 'unmarried' is a belief which goes hand in hand with understanding English. So if it is a belief at all, it is one which is inextricably connected with understanding a language, and this, surely, is simply to be describing a semantic connection under another name.

To conclude this chapter, we can offer, tentatively, an amended version of Putnam's criterion for analyticity. We will say that the relation between lexical items X and Y is analytic if and only if:

(i) X entails Y;
(ii) It is not possible to consistently imagine a situation in which X does not entail Y;
(iii) Y provides a necessary condition for being X;
(iv) native speakers can and do use Y as a (partial) criterion for being X.

No doubt this could be expressed more concisely, but it is as well to spell out the various factors involved.

Notice that although Y will be in some sense part of the meaning of X in the cases where they are analytically related, it will not be the whole story about the meaning of X. Y provides only a necessary condition for X and so it is perfectly possible for something to be Y without being X. It is, for example, a necessary condition for something being a nightmare that it should be a dream. But not every dream is a nightmare. This leaves us with a further problem, then, to which we shall return. For if these analytic relations between words do not provide a full account of their meaning, we ought to look for something else which, either alone or in conjunction, does.

Notes

1. See for example McCawley (1968a,b), Lakoff (1971, 1972) as well as the articles by McCawley and others in Seuren (ed.) (1974).

The use of semantic primitives, or something equivalent to them, is not restricted to these writers, or to the others mentioned in the text. Linguists working within such diverse traditions as Bendix (1966), Bierwisch (1971), Fillmore (1971), Leech (1974), Lehrer (1974) and Nida (1975a,b) all endorse the use of such elements. Psychologists, too (Miller and Johnson-Laird 1976; Clark and Clark 1977) have advanced theories which depend on breaking down words into smaller elements (though the former in particular, attempt some independent account of the resulting atomic components). The use and endorsement of semantic primitives as a method of semantic description is widespread in artificial intelligence (e.g. Schank (1972, 1975); Wilks (1972, 1977a); Norman and Rumelhart (1975), whether they are claimed to have psychological plausibility (by Schank, in particular) or to be merely a useful engineering device (as in Wilks 1977a, at least).

To claim engineering utility insulates a proposal against theoretical objections. Nevertheless, it is worth pointing out that even if primitives are regarded (as suggested later) as a sublanguage of English (as Wilks regards his) then the inadequacy of most of such examples of analysis is clear too. Wilks analyses the psychological sense of 'grasp' as

(((*ANI SUBJ)(SIGN OBJE)((THIS(MAN PART)INST)((SAME SIGN)(TRUE BE)(THINK)))

which he glosses as

> (this).... implies that grasping is a THINKing action, that the SAME SIGN is TRUE, an action preferably done by an ANImate agent to a SIGN (the same sign as earlier) OBJEct, and with an INSTrument that is a particular PART of a MAN ... (1977b:6)

Ignoring the fact that the gloss seems to misrepresent the intention of the original by placing TRUE outside the scope of THINK (not everything we think is true), there is nothing in the analysis itself to preclude the possibility that people might think with their feet (or any other MAN PART). This seems to miss something quite central to this sense of 'grasp'.

2. It seems to me that Chomsky is not entirely accurate in his discussion of this requirement, which as a methodological stance is consistent with, though less ambitious than his own position. For example in Chomsky (1980:71) he says that Foster's (1976:2) admittedly inelegant formulation

> amounts to the injunction that we should not try to formulate the grammar that a person implicitly knows (so we claim), but rather to state the facts that he explicitly knows

But this is not so: the injunction is that we should try to formulate a grammar which is such that if a person explicitly knew it, he could behave in the same way vis-à-vis the ability described by it as does the person who (so we might then go on to claim) knows that grammar implicitly. This amounts to exactly the same requirement of precision and testability of grammatical statements as is insisted on by Chomsky, and for Foster is the only way of making sense of claims about 'tacit knowledge'. He would presumably be reluctant to go on to make such a claim. I agree with Chomsky that when verbal quibbles about what constitutes knowledge are out of the way this is a claim which is unobjectionable and that Foster is wrong to be so reluctant. But I do not think that Foster is suggesting that the proper object of linguistic inquiry is a person's conscious knowledge of his language.

3. This is the '-en' of 'redden', not of 'written', of course.

4. It is presumably a factual question as to whether such enrichment actually does make a properly formulated semantics impossible. It may be that the austerity which Evans and McDowell, along with other Davidsonians, regard as desirable in a semantic theory (it is not supposed to use any semantic concepts other than that of truth), would make such an enrichment impossible, where a less stringent approach allowing notions like possible worlds could produce a semantics for these elements satisfying the remaining criteria of any such theory. Dowty (1979) attempts to provide a semantics for elements such as CAUSE and BECOME within the framework of Montague grammar. If such a programme could be carried out for the full range of semantic atoms offered by their proponents then there could be no objection to them on the present grounds.

5. Examples (5) and (6) are for illustration only. See J.A. Fodor (1972) for some criticisms of Davidson's (1967a) analysis of adverbs. Although I assume that a recursive characterisation of truth will play a large part in the semantic description of a language, I would not wish to be taken as committed to Davidson's particular

proposals in this area.

6. Although we have not been concerned with psychological interpretations of definition-based theories, it is worth pointing out that no experimental support is forthcoming here: J.A. Fodor *et al.* (1980).

3 NAÏVE METAPHYSICS

I

What questions should a theory of word meaning attempt to answer? A traditional requirement is that, given the lexicon of some natural language, it should show how the semantic combination rules of the language operate with the lexicon in such a way that the following pairs of sentences are shown to be related to each other by entailment:

(1) a Joe persuaded Jim to leave
    b Jim intends to leave
(2) a Joe persuaded Jim that the earth was flat
    b Jim believes that the earth is flat
(3) a Tiddles is a cat
    b Tiddles is an animal
(4) a I have a toothache
    b I have a pain
(5) a Bill had a nightmare
    b Bill had a dream
(6) a The brick is red
    b The brick is coloured

In what follows, we shall have nothing further to say about the details of such a combinatorial mechanism, but will assume that once given the system of semantic relations existing between items in a lexicon, it is possible to construct one.

From our point of view, there are more fundamental questions which a theory of word meaning should settle first. If it is to count as a response to Quine's indeterminacy thesis, then such a theory should show that when we think we are referring to an enduring physical object, that is indeed what we are referring to, rather than any of the exotic alternative possibilities we discussed. But even if we can show this to be the case, that is still not the whole story. Chomsky (1965: 201; 1976:44; 1980:62) has pointed out that the notion of a 'nameable object' is itself very complex. Not any lump of physical matter or collection of lumps of physical matter is naturally nameable. It is surely a basic requirement of an adequate theory of word meaning that it should provide an account of what constitutes a 'nameable thing'. Clearly, not every nameable thing will actually have a proper name, but we are interested in the distinction between those things which do not have a proper name but which could have if the need arose, and those things which could not naturally have a proper name. (This is not to say that they are not capable of being referred to, or described in some other way. There is a trivial sense in which anything at all is nameable, for we can always produce an identifying definite description of sufficient detail to pick out what we want to.)

If we have an answer to this question we can progress to the next one, the question of the way the world is divided up by the vocabulary of a language: what sort of things are seen as sufficiently similar to fall under the same term, and which things as different. In other words, how do we classify or form categories. To some (most notably Whorf 1956) it has seemed that this dividing up of the world is essentially arbitrary, governed only by social or cultural utility. But this arbitrariness has limits: it is, we assume, *things* which are grouped together, not parts of things or collections of parts of things, even for Whorf. It is an empirical matter as to how arbitrary the parcelling up of the world by language actually is: in the few domains in which cross-cultural comparisons are possible, notably colour and shape, a consensus seems to be emerging that a good deal of the arbitrariness is only apparent and that there are fairly severe psychological or neurophysiological constraints on the possibilities available to us (Berlin and Kay 1969; Rosch 1973). It seems to me that questions of this sort are also the legitimate province of a theory of word meaning: alongside questions such as 'what counts as a nameable object (or action, or event)?' we must also ask 'by what criteria are groups of objects, actions or events classified together, regarded as falling under the same term?'.

Some simple observations suggest further questions which a theory of word meaning should be addressed to. It is well known that to assign a word to a syntactic category is only in small part to suggest its general semantic properties (i.e. those which it shares with other members of that category). We saw in the preceding chapter that there was good reason to suspect that the syntactic category of nouns contains several subcategories which can be distinguished from each other in terms of their semantic behaviour (nouns like 'cat' as opposed to nouns like 'bachelor', for example). The same is true of other nouns. 'Coal' is a noun and so in some of its uses is 'nothing', but the semantic principles by which they are interpreted are utterly different. There are also syntactic differences between them, of course, in terms of the range of structures in which they can appear, but nothing which would motivate our assigning them to two semantically relevant separate syntactic categories.

While on syntactic grounds 'begin' and 'decapitate' might both be classed as verbs, the semantic properties of the first are quite different from those of the second. Again, there are also co-occurrence differences between these two, but nothing which is systematically relatable to their semantic properties. Most adjectives have more in common with each other semantically than they do with prepositions, but there are still semantic differences between adjectives which are obscured by apparent similarity in other respects. Adjectives like 'valuable' and 'fake' do not differ syntactically from each other in any interesting or revealing way, but their semantic behaviour is very different.

(7) a This is a valuable Picasso   entails   This is a Picasso
    b This is a fake Picasso   does not entail   This is a Picasso

Conversely, adjectives which do differ syntactically may not differ semantically

(8) a John is likely (*probable) to come
    b It is likely (probable) that John will come

As well as belonging to syntactic categories, then, words are also placed in semantic categories. Semantic categories contain groups of words which may or may not be syntactically alike, but which share in large part their semantic properties: behaving similarly in inference, having similar kinds of criteria for their truth or falsity, or even perhaps by deriving their meaning from a certain type of analytic definition.

It seems obvious that if these semantic groupings or categories are systematic, then a descriptively adequate linguistic theory should provide an enumeration of at least the major types (which are presumably universal), and provide a complete list from which each language might draw in a way perhaps analogous to the role of phonological theory with respect to distinctive features. And such a theory ought to go beyond merely enumerating the categories, towards a description of the semantic or logical properties belonging to each, again presumably universal. The process of learning a word in a language must involve placing it in the appropriate semantic category, as well as in the correct syntactic category. In both cases a number of other properties of the word will then be 'known' without further experience, as a consequence of the general properties of the categories into which it has been placed. Learning the meaning of a word involves both universal and particular grammar, if this is correct.

It is an open question of course whether this is ultimately a feasible project: it might turn out, for example, that we have to admit as many semantic categories as there are individual words, which would show that we were wrong in initially hypothesising that there was a level of abstraction at which words could be said to behave similarly, semantically speaking. As for syntax, it is a question of homing in on the appropriate level of idealisation: if by ignoring individual idiosyncrasies, or even sub-regularities, we can still state principles which seem to give us some insight and to be accurate over a reasonably wide domain, then we are justified in taking a more panoramic view and ignoring individual details and exceptions. The fact that in syntax we may not have a totally satisfactory distributional definition of noun, verb, etc. does not prevent us from stating significant and revealing generalisations in terms of nouns and verbs.

At various points the last two types of question – the nature of classification and semantic categories – overlap. For example, the work of Kripke (1972) and Putnam (1975b) can be seen in part as an attempt to provide an analysis of the semantic category of 'proper name' and 'natural kind word': to discover what their logical and linguistic properties are. But analysis of the properties of natural kind words involves discovering what sort of principles govern the membership of a natural kind: to anticipate, their answer is that it is the presumed sharing of some essential 'inner constitution'. What makes something a member of a natural kind is that it shares the same essential properties (which may not actually be known) as the original or sample members of the kind. As well as casting light on the logic of our use of this kind of term, this answer can be seen as a contribution towards the discovery of the principles by which things are grouped together into categories, for here we have a case where superficial appearance, or the satisfaction of a particular definition, is not alone criterial for membership in a particular category. In general it seems likely that there will turn out to be close interactions between the following questions:

(i) Principles of individuation – what is a 'nameable thing'?
(ii) Principles of categorisation – what governs the grouping

together of 'things' under the same term?
(iii) Semantic categories — what are the semantically significant groupings of words in natural languages and what properties do each of these groupings have?

A satisfactory theory of word meaning should provide some sort of answer to all three of these questions. It should probably do a lot more, besides, but these are the only questions with which we shall concern ourselves here. Question (i) will be taken up immediately: the rest of this chapter presents a first try at stating such principles of nameability, and also tries to develop a descriptive framework within which to discuss categorisation. Some possible principles of categorisation and their implications for word meaning will be discussed in Chapters 4 and 5. Discussion of semantic categories and their properties will be for the most part delayed until the final chapter.

II

First, let us concentrate on the notion 'physical object'. The sense of 'physical object' which concerns us is intended to be neutral as between 'things' and 'stuff', and is in implicit opposition to the notion 'abstract object', though the term is used in different ways by, for example, Chomsky, when he says

> the most 'elementary' notion we have, the notion 'physical object' ... seems to be quite complex. ... One wing of an aeroplane is an object, but its left half, though equally continuous, is not. (1976:203)

In my sense, the left half of the wing of an aeroplane is certainly a physical object, whereas an idea or a joke is not. What Chomsky means is that it is not a naturally 'nameable thing', and for this notion I shall use the term 'nameable'. 'Nameable' is obviously a language dependent notion, 'physical object' is not. It might make sense to ask whether an animal has the same notion of physical object as we do, but it cannot make sense to ask if an animal has the same notion of nameable as us.[1]

There have been various philosophical and linguistic speculations as to what the criterial features of a physical object might be, ranging from relative permanence or stability through time (this seems to be one way of understanding the relevance of Wittgenstein's disappearing chair (1972: para. 80, Chomsky (1976:45)) to homogeneity and detachability from surroundings (Quine 1971:146) and so on. These speculations seem to presuppose the prior general criterion of observability: abstract objects are not observable, physical objects are, at least in principle. Certain kinds of subatomic particles might be problematic here, and a fuller account would say something about audibility (are noises physical objects?), but observability is a good beginning. (It certainly seems obvious that 'physical object' is a notion intimately related to perception even though not necessarily wholly reconstructible in purely phenomenal terms.)

It nevertheless seems that to adopt observability alone as a criterion for physical object is at once too weak and too strong. It is too weak because hallucinations or the results of various illusions (holograms or tricks with mirrors) are observable but we would not want to say that they were physical objects. It is perhaps too strong in that air is not observable but we would not therefore want to say that it was an abstract object. What we need to do is to distinguish more clearly the scientist's sense of physical object, by which air and illusions and perhaps even hallucinations are physical objects, in the sense that they have a physical explanation, from the everyday sense we are interested in, the sense of 'naive physics',[2] or perhaps 'naive metaphysics', in which they are not physical objects. In many cases there is a clash between what science tells us – air is a physical object – and what naive untutored observation tells us – air is not a physical object.

This done, we can see that the necessary supplementation is achieved by adding to observability the requirement that something which is a physical object can also be touched, again, at least in principle. This connection between visibility and touchability (or perhaps better 'feelability' – you can, technically speaking, touch air, though it is not 'feelable' in the sense intended) seems to be particularly central to our notion of physical object, and to be a connection which is not learned (see below). It is not a logical connection either, for as we have seen, not everything visible is touchable.

Let us assume that the features of observability, touchability, (relative) permanence and detachability are an accurate if not exhaustive account of the properties of our naive concept of physical object. Over recent years there has accumulated a fair amount of experimental evidence concerning what is of course a fundamental question of cognitive psychology: how do we acquire this concept? Much of this evidence confirms what we might already have suspected: that at various stages in the early life of a child it is possible to see the emergence of the ability to make a set of discriminations among percepts which can be jointly taken to be characteristic of physical objects, and that the nature of our perceptual system and its organisation is such that we cannot help developing such a concept. This is not to say that the concept of a physical object is completely innate in its fully formed version: the situation is much more interesting and complex than that. We will turn to a brief review of the relevant evidence.

Bower, on whose work I rely throughout (Bower 1974, 1977, 1979), has discovered that newborn children assume the connection mentioned above between visibility and touchability, and also assume (wrongly, as it turns out) that the connection is invariant. (Ideas that are innate are not necessarily correct ideas.) Discussing the reaching behaviour of newborn babies, Bower concludes

> The baby acts as if he knows that an object he sees can be touched (1977:31)

(It also appears, incidentally, that newborn children assume that there is a connection between visibility and audibility: that where there is a noise, there is a visibile object that is its source. This is again a connection which does not have to be learned.) Up to the age of six months, phenomena which defy the connection between visibility and touchability are simply mysterious to babies — such a thing is an 'impossible concept' for them at this stage, and they display the surprise and confusion one might expect under such circumstances. Bower describes how children will repeatedly reach in astonishment for objects which they can see but which are 'not there' — optical illusions experimentally induced. At the age of eight or nine months, however, the child seems to discover that real and illusory objects of the type concerned behave differently as regards binocular and motion parallax (the apparent change of position or direction of an object against its background detectable both from the fact that our vision is binocular and via motion of the head). Thus the child has learned that, contrary to first expectations, to be visible is not always to be touchable, but that objects which are both visible and touchable also bear predictable relationships to their surroundings and background, via parallax.

Motion and binocular parallax are used to compute both distance and trajectory and it seems that the ability to do this is present from birth, though it improves during the first few months of life. I take it that the effect of this calculation of distance and position relative to background is to provide the basis for the property of 'detachability from surroundings' which is claimed to be a part of the concept of a physical object. This matter is clearly more complex, as 'surroundings' are presumably also physical objects, but it seems safe to conclude that this aspect of physical object is reducible to perceptual factors of this sort. It also seems clear that some of the concepts involved in nameability are beginning to emerge here: 'detachability from surroundings' suggests the idea of a self-contained individual object, as opposed to some arbitrary lump of the physical. The same remarks apply to the concept of the permanence of objects (relatively speaking, of course) — that an object can be recognised as identical with itself over time and space. Wittgenstein's chair example trades on this concept, which has been much studied and is also a complicated affair. Interpretations differ over the significance of experimental results but the general picture seems to be something like this: at the age of about five months, babies regard a moving object appearing at various places as the same object, though before this it seems that they do not (Turner 1975:76; though see Bower 1979:147). By the time the child is a year old, however, he has acquired fully the concept of the permanence of objects, however this is done — memory development must clearly play a crucial part — and this concept seems to come to have the same status as the connection between visibility and touchability has in very early life — namely that of a conceptual necessity. Bower (1977:52) describes how babies of various ages reacted to the sight of objects which appeared to melt away softly and silently like mist (achieved with mirrors and lights). Young babies showed no surprise or interest in this phenomenon: it presumably is not yet ruled out for them that physical objects should not behave in this way. Babies of a year old however apparently found it impossible to believe what they had seen, inspecting the box and searching for the object which they had just seen disappear, not being satisfied until they found the object. A physical object behaving in this way seems to be an 'impossible concept' for them: they have learned that physical objects do not behave like Wittgenstein's chair.

While this is a rather cursory treatment of a complex and interesting topic, it seems safe to conclude that we can identify the point at which the child has a concept of physical object, and trace its development in part from various features, either present at birth or acquired automatically during maturation, connected with the perceptual and cognitive equipment of human beings.

The concept of physical object for the child at this point involves at least the notions of observability and feelability, relative permanence through space and time, and potential detachability from surroundings.

Notice that the first two properties would only distinguish a notion of 'the physical', strictly speaking, as opposed to that of an individual physical object: but the latter two seem to require that a particular lump of the physical be identified as the same lump; i.e. it is regarded as an individual.

A stubborn Quinean might at this point ask how we know that these various perceptually based features combine to form *this* concept and not some logically possible and coextensive one. We will return later to a different answer to this question, but for the time being it is sufficient to point out that this notion of physical object has been identified independently of any linguistic investigation, and that the hypothesis that the child operates, after a time, with such a notion is not indeterminate, if the arguments of the first chapter are correct, but just the simplest hypothesis consistent both with our observation of the child's behaviour and with independently supported hypotheses about perception.

III

In English, as in other languages, evidence for what is regarded as a nameable comes from various syntactic or semantic devices of reference and quantification: by and large, things which have proper names, and things which can be referred to by a singular non-collective countable noun (and hence can acceptably appear in the plural) are *ipso facto* regarded as nameables. Even this is too strong, really, for absolutely anything can be called a 'thing' and so by this criterion would count as a nameable. But the general idea is clear.

It is obvious that not everything physical is regarded as a nameable in this sense: the left half of an aeroplane wing, water, wine and gold, for example. (Equally, not everything so nameable is a physical object, but we will put aside here consideration of abstract objects and such like.) We do not regard the sum total of denotata of mass terms as nameables, even though there is no logical reason why we should not, as Quine (1960) and Goodman (1951) have argued (see also Lyons 1977: 226). The notion of a single but scattered object of which particular samples of gold or water are parts is not self-contradictory. And Chomsky has pointed out that although some collections of objects are regarded as nameables, not every conceivable type of collection can be so regarded there are no logical grounds for the apparent non-existence in natural languages of words such as 'LIMB', similar to 'limb' except that it designates the single object consisting of a dog's four legs so that 'its LIMB is brown' (like 'its head is brown') would mean that the object consisting of the four legs is brown. Similarly, there is no a priori reason why a natural language could not contain a word 'HERD' like the collective 'herd' except that it denotes a single scattered object with cows as parts, so that 'a cow lost a leg' implies 'the HERD lost a leg' etc. (1965:201)

If Chomsky is correct, then there must be some descriptive principles — principles of nameability — which dictate that 'HERD' is not a 'natural' word. But in order to be able to begin to formulate these principles, we need some neutral metalanguage with which to talk about those bits of the physical concerned, independently of whether they are nameable or not.

When talking about categories and collections of objects the natural metalanguage to use as a starting point is set theory. But in talking about objects and parts of objects set theory does not seem appropriate: we want to say somehow that every thing that is in the extension of 'finger' is also in the extension of 'hand'. Associating extensions with sets in the usual way would mean expressing this as something like 'every X which is a member of the set of fingers, is also a member of the set of hands'. And if taken literally, this does not seem right (see Leonard and Goodman 1940:45) for fingers are not members of the set of hands — hands are. We would have to take X as ranging over lumps of flesh, cells or atoms, or some other artificial alternative in order to make sense of such a claim. But that is not what we wanted: what we really ought to be doing is saying that everything that is a finger is also part of a hand. The metalanguage we will use enables us to do just this. It derives from the 'calculus of individuals' developed by Leonard and Goodman. (Their purposes were rather different, concerned with a philosophical objection to the notion of class or set as the basis for mathematics, but that does not detract from the usefulness of their calculus for other purposes. For discussion of the philosophical motivation of the calculus, see Benacerraf and Putnam 1964:21-5.)

This metalanguage uses the usual resources of the predicate calculus as regards connectives and quantifiers. Its variables are x, y, z..., which range over individuals, here understood to be physical objects in the sense in which both aeroplanes and the left half of an aeroplane wing are physical objects. In addition it has a primitive predicate 'O' (for 'overlaps') understood in the sense of Goodman (1951):

> Two individuals overlap if they have some common content, whether or not either is wholly contained in the other (p. 48)

O is symmetric, reflexive and intransitive. With O we can define, following Goodman in most respects, various other predicates and functions:

(1) $D(x, y) =_{df} \sim O(x, y)$ (Discrete from)

(2) $P(x, y) =_{df} (\forall z)(O(z, x) \rightarrow O(z, y))$ (Part of)

(3) $PP(x, y) =_{df} P(x, y) \wedge \sim P(y, x)$ (Proper part of)

(4) $x = y =_{df} (\forall z)(O(z, x) \leftrightarrow O(z, y))$ (Identity)

(5) $PR(x, y) =_{df} (\iota z)[(\forall w)(P(w, z) \leftrightarrow P(w, x) \wedge P(w, y))]$
(read ιz as 'the unique z such that ...')
(Product or common part of two overlapping individuals)

(6) $SUM(x, y) =_{df} (\iota z)[(\forall w)(D(w, z) \leftrightarrow D(w, x) \wedge D(w, y))]$
(Sum of two individuals)

There are several things to notice about these definitions. First, it is PP which corresponds (to some extent) with our usual notion of 'part of', not P. Secondly, only two individuals which overlap have a product. Thirdly, any two individuals have a sum, defined as that (possibly composite, possibly scattered) individual which is such that everything discrete from its components is discrete from it, and vice versa. (If this definition seems puzzling at first it might be useful to point out that it is the 'only if' part of the biconditional that does most of the work.) Thus we now have a way of talking about scattered individuals, parts of individuals, agglomerations of parts of individuals and other bizarre phenomena in a reasonably precise way, and we can turn to the question of which of these are regarded as naturally nameable. The way in which we shall approach this is to ask which of the types of individual describable in the calculus under the interpretation we have given it could be nameable, and then to ask what property, formal or intuitive, distinguishes this type of individual from others.

Notice that in the calculus as Goodman describes it, and as we are using it here, the term 'individual' carries no suggestion of particularity or continuity, but merely means whatever the variables of the calculus range over, in our case physical objects, or better, 'lumps of the physical':

an individual need not be organized or uniform, need not be continuous or have regular boundaries (p. 36)

Clearly, then, not everything which counts as an individual in this sense is nameable. At the very least though, we might suppose, an individual which *is* continuous and which *does* have boundaries is nameable. This is perhaps what Russell meant when he claimed that

> (names designate)... some definite continuous portion of space time (1940:91)

Let us adopt this suggestion as our first, and arguably most basic, principle. We perhaps need to add the further condition that the individual must also be relatively homogeneous in composition, though this is clearly more relevant for natural objects than man-made ones:

(N1) Individuals which are (relatively homogeneous), continuous and bounded are nameable.

This is a sufficient condition only and is pretty liberal, not distinguishing between puddles, raindrops, hairs, lumps of putty, people or planets, though the relative likelihoods of each of them being bearers of a name varies extremely. (For a discussion of some of the social or utilitarian factors involved in this variation see Strawson 1974:42ff.) There is a good sense in which this type of nameable is most basic to us: it is based on those perceptual discriminations eventuating in the child's conception of a bounded, continuous, enduring physical object as discussed earlier; and other nameables are either combinations (sums) or subparts of these. We will refer to individuals which satisfy (N1) as 'N1 nameables'.

Spatiotemporal continuity alone is not a sufficient condition for nameability, as Chomsky's (1976:203) wing example demonstrates. The left half of an aeroplane wing is spatiotemporally continuous but does not seem naturally nameable. The individual in question is a proper part of the wing, and both it and the wing are proper parts of the aeroplane (and of countless other individuals which are the sum of the aeroplane and some different individual). Why are some proper parts nameable and others apparently not? The answer seems clear enough when we consider the proper parts of the aeroplane that are nameable: wings, tail, cabin, etc.: they each have some characteristic function and, in this case, a characteristic shape. These features seem sufficient for something to count as a nameable subpart.

But some proper parts that do not have a characteristic function or shape are also nameable: moles, freckles, stripes and stains, for example. Clearly what they have in common is that they stand out from their background in some way. In general it seems to be the case that

(N2) An individual which is a proper part of an N1 nameable is itself nameable if and only if it has a characteristic function, appearance, or behaviour.

Whereas the content of (N1) might be described as psychological, in that it attempts to capture the gestalt properties of nameables, that of (N2) is, as far as function is concerned at least, more properly described as social, in individual cases, if not as a general principle. The factors which make for a characteristic function can be quite variable, and in the limiting case might depend on very culture specific and idiosyncratic facts. Take as an example words for parts of the body: hands, knees and suchlike have characteristic shapes and functions and are invariably named, but many areas of the body do not, and are not named: the area which might be described as the 'middle third of the underneath of the forearm', for example. But in a society among whom there is a powerful myth concerning that particular region of the forearm, or for whom it had some other special salience, there would presumably be a name for it.

The preceding discussion has already made it clear that the notion of a nameable is intimately connected with complex systems of beliefs about the provenance of things, their relation to each other, their possible functions, their appearance and so on. To an austerely minded linguist it might seem that we were much too liberal in using these notions in framing (N2). We might learn more about the concept of a nameable, it could be argued, by not taking these notions for granted, but exploring each of them on its own. We could ask what exactly is involved in the notion of something fulfilling a certain function, or having a certain appearance. We do not have to travel far down this road, though, before it becomes apparent that these notions are not actually independent of that of a nameable: it is not possible to conceive of a function and its fulfilment without having the concept of a thing — a nameable — to fulfil it, or a thing which is the result of its being fulfilled. This does not make the mention of function in (N2) and below, in (N3), circular, necessarily, for in both cases where it is mentioned it is against the background of objects which could already have been singled out as nameables on the basis of (N1): other functionally salient individuals are either parts of or collections of such objects. It does however mean that there is little chance of reducing the concept of a nameable completely to antecedently understood less complex notions. It seems likely that notions such as 'nameable', 'function', 'appearance' and so on are like 'analyticity', 'synonymity' and 'meaning': a set of concepts which are ultimately interdependent in such a way that an attempt to define each of them presupposes an understanding of the others.

In the calculus of individuals, any two individuals have a sum, which is in turn an individual.[3] In the cases where the resulting individual is widely scattered and disparate, as in Goodman's example:

If the Arctic sea and a speck of dust in the Sahara are individuals, then their sum is an individual (p. 36)

then it seems very unlikely to be nameable. Nevertheless, as Chomsky has emphasised, some such scattered individuals are nameable. The individuals need not under certain conditions be spatiotemporally continuous: we can still regard a fence as a single object even if it has a few breaks in it, or if it consists of a row of unconnected stakes. Similarly, certain constellations of stars (the Plough, etc.) can be regarded as nameables (Strawson 1961:83), as can groups of buildings, collections of trees and so on. It seems that there are various factors involved here. One factor is the relative constancy of the spatiotemporal relations the various components of the nameable bear to each other, that is, spatiotemporal contiguity (in the sense of 'neighbouring' rather than 'touching'). Bits of a fence separated by long stretches of space or time are not regarded as belonging to the same nameable. The example of constellations demonstrates that it is *relative* spatiotemporal contiguity that is relevant (cf. Sampson 1980:41). If the stars making up the Plough wandered the heavens separately from each other we would not regard them as united in one thing (though we might if their wanderings were restricted to a fixed portion of the sky and did not intermingle with other stars). A collection of buildings have to be fairly close to each other, relative to their surroundings, if they are to count as a village or a town. But although relative spatiotemporal contiguity can be a sufficient condition for the status of a collection of objects as a nameable, it is not usually the only one. At least two other factors are involved: the fact that a human (or animal) agency has been involved can cause us to view several scattered objects as making up a nameable, when we would not otherwise. Hadrian's wall, for example, is incomplete for long stretches. Artistic creations like the notorious Tate Gallery bricks or ancient collections of large stones likewise are nameables; Chomsky's own example here is that of a deliberately arranged collection of leaves on a tree (1976:44) (though leaves are not N1 nameables). Artistic creations are presumably the limiting case of this type of thing, and it is arguable that some of these are in any case achieving what effect they have precisely by transgressing the bounds of the natural. But in general it seems to be true that something which is seen as the product of an intentional act is a nameable.

A further condition which is sufficient for nameability is if a collection of things jointly fulfil a function which is not completely served by any of them separately. That collection can then be regarded as a nameable: 'fence' could again be a suitable example here. That this requirement is independent of human agency is demonstrated by the fact that what we take to be a naturally occurring row of 'stakes' could legitimately be individuated as a fence provided it fulfilled that function, but there is no human agency involved here. We can state what distinguishes nameable from non-nameable sums as follows:

N(3) A sum of N1 nameables is itself nameable if they are (relatively) spatiotemporally contiguous or the product of human (or animal?) agency or jointly fulfil a function not served by any of them separately.

The type of example covered by (N3) includes Stonehenge, bikinis, cars, skeletons and towns.

We must of course distinguish between things which are regarded as single objects even though physically consisting of separate objects, and things which are designated by singular count nouns or proper names but nevertheless regarded as plural: collective words like 'herd', 'pile' and 'flock', and proper names like 'the United States' or 'the Commonwealth'. As a matter of fact, for some collective terms spatiotemporal contiguity again seems to be important: a group of cattle or sheep must not be too widely dispersed if they are to count as a herd or a flock. But there is a good deal more looseness here, which seems fairly exactly correlated with what we might call the 'degree of analyticity' involved: the Commonwealth or the United States of America are pretty widely dispersed, and it seems clear that this sort of institutional name has a descriptive, definitional or analytic content which is not appropriately handled in the terms we have been using. Football teams, for example, only meet the conditions of (N3) (if then) when actually playing, but no one would want to say that the team ceased to exist at other times, when the members are widely dispersed. It is a matter of legislation, in the widest sense, as to what these institutional names refer to.

The question of nameable scattered objects has provoked some discussion. Chomsky (1965:29) claimed that

> terms designating objects ... must designate objects meeting a condition of spatiotemporal contiguity

though a footnote from which we quoted above suggests that he does not intend this to apply to 'more abstract and functionally defined notions' such as some of those we have just been describing. It is not clear whether Chomsky means 'touching' or 'neighbouring' by 'contiguity' here: Sampson (1980:40) takes him to mean 'touching' and offers a counterexample:

> the French singular noun 'rouage', which designates the object consisting of the roadwheels of a vehicle and is thus a very close match to Chomsky's allegedly impossible LIMB.

Sampson writes:

> Chomsky has told me in correspondence that he does not regard 'rouage' as a genuine counterexample to ... [the claim quoted above] ... because it does not designate 'a scattered object in ... the sense of the calculus of individuals. Thus, the left half of the front wheel and the middle of the back wheel do not constitute a part of the 'rouage''. (p. 41)

Sampson finds Chomsky's reply unconvincing, saying that he can imagine talking about these segments collectively as 'the rusty part of the "rouage"'.

At the risk of adding further misunderstanding to this exchange, it seems to me that neither participant is quite correct. Chomsky's original footnote exempting functionally defined nameables from contiguity in the strict sense — if that is what he intended — is sufficient to preserve his claim (which corresponds in part to our (N1)). What would be needed as a counterexample would be a nameable non-contiguous sum which was not individuated by function (or, presumably, by agency). Sampson's 'rouage' seems pretty clearly a case which is individuated by function ('undercarriage' might be a similar example), and falls under (N3): it is therefore only a counterexample if Chomsky did not intend to exclude functionally defined nameables.

On the other hand, Chomsky's claim that 'rouage' does not designate a genuine scattered individual in the sense of the calculus seems incorrect: each wheel is an individual and so there is an individual which is the sum of the wheels. What Chomsky perhaps means is that in the case of these scattered nameables, the calculus of individuals relation 'proper part of' does not always coincide with our intuitive notion 'part of' (which is not surprising, given that the notion of 'individual' in the calculus is so far from our intuitive one). This is certainly so for the case he describes: I do not find Sampson's claim plausible that he could refer to this collection of wheel segments by a singular count noun; we would surely refer to the rusty parts of the rouage. The various relations that 'part of' subsumes in English require considerable analysis (see Cruse 1979 for some interesting examples and discussion), but in the cases we have been looking at it seems generally to be the case that PP(x, y) corresponds to 'part of' only when (1) x is an N2 nameable and y is an N1 or N2 nameable, or (2) y is an N3 nameable sum and x is an N1 or N2 nameable. A wheel is part of a 'rouage', and part of a wheel is part of a 'rouage', but the individual consisting of a spoke from each wheel is not a nameable, and therefore not a part of the 'rouage' (except in the technical calculus sense captured by P).

Let us return to Chomsky's HERD and LIMB. A HERD is 'a single scattered object with cows as parts' so that 'a cow lost a leg' implies 'the HERD lost a leg' (p. 201). (N3) will account for the non-existence of such a word, for the relative contiguity condition holds only for 'herd', not HERD, and neither the joint function nor human agency requirements are fulfilled. Of course, if things were arranged so that any of these conditions did obtain, then (N3) claims that a word having the properties of HERD could exist. Perhaps Chomsky's leaf arranger might eventually, bored with the limitations of his medium, turn to arranging cattle and produce as his latest exhibit a HERD of which he might say 'unfortunately one of the cows had an accident and so my HERD has a leg missing'. We could probably also tell a similar story about joint function: I have read that a sufficiently dense population of pigs has the property that it will thoroughly dig over and manure a piece of ground in the course of rooting for food. The well organised smallholder can, by moving his pigs around, have all his digging done for him without effort. Now, suppose one smallholder rents out his collection of pigs, which he calls the SNOUT, for this purpose. Then he might say, after the SNOUT has encountered a particularly rocky field 'My SNOUT has a sore nose today'.

(N3) does not seem sufficient to rule out Chomsky's other example, LIMB, where LIMB designates the single object consisting of a dog's four legs. The legs satisfy the condition of contiguity and it is arguable that they also satisfy the joint function condition: in the letter at least, for four legs hold a dog up, whereas one leg, unless the creature is phenomenally acrobatic, will not. We might conclude from this that it is genuinely just an accident that there is no word such as LIMB, bearing roughly the same relation to 'dog' as 'rouage' does to the vehicle it is part of. However, there is a difference between LIMB and 'rouage' which seems to be significant: the components of a 'rouage' are N1 nameables — wheels, spokes, etc., which, though not all very useful on their own, are independent of the 'rouage' in principle. But the components of a LIMB are not independent of 'dog' in the same way: they are N2 nameables. It may be that the difference largely coincides with that between naturally occurring organic wholes and artefactual objects: a 'rouage' is assembled from its independently fabricated bits, a dog is not. But at any rate, it seems that the conditions on nameability of sums of N2 nameables involve something like the 'touching' sense of contiguity: we have the word 'hand' for the sum of fingers, thumb and palm, but we have no word for the sum of fingers and toes, or of wrist and ankle. (Some languages have terms which can mean either finger *or* toe, or wrist *or* ankle, but that is a different matter: the word only refers to one at a time.)

(N4) A sum of N2 nameables is nameable only if the individuals making up the sum are adjacent to each other.

(N4) will rule out an example like LIMB. It also implies that an expression like 'the rusty part of the rouage' can only refer to a continuous stretch of the rouage, and that when the smallholder says that his SNOUT has a sore nose, he is referring only to a single nose, not the sum of all the noses belonging to the SNOUT. These implications accord with my intuitions, but it remains to be seen to what extent (N4), and (N1)-(N3), actually achieve observational adequacy for other cases: they must be regarded as first approximations at this stage.

IV

The principles of nameability just sketched are actually fairly liberal, as liberal as the range of forms that nature, human agency and function can distinguish. Notice in particular that any detachable, or bounded, continuous lump of stuff is nameable. This seems correct, for even continuous stretches of the substances picked out by mass terms can be nameable: lakes, particular objects of gold, grain or butter. Nevertheless, it is true that most such lumps are not in fact named and it is natural to ask why this is so.

The syntactically defined category of mass terms corresponds to several semantically relevant dimensions. One of the most important is that of shape, or rather, the lack of it: a sufficient condition for being designated by a mass term is lack of a characteristic shape. This is not to say that instances of what is designated by a mass term have no shape at all — whatever that would be like — or that they are amorphous or have only a vague shape (see Lyons 1977:277). Pieces of metal have clear and determinate shapes and so do liquids: usually the shape of their container, but none of these has a *characteristic* or essential shape: we cannot talk of or imagine a water-shape or a gold-shape. The same seems to be true even for cases of terms which can be used as either countable or mass terms: 'a fish' has a characteristic shape, 'some fish', in the non-plural sense intended, does not. Here it seems to be the countable sense of 'fish' which is primary. When a word which is primarily a mass term is used countably, it does not thereby take a shape: 'fog' lacks a characteristic shape, but so does 'a fog' as in 'there was a bad fog yesterday'. Such uses are of course understood as 'an instance of . . . ', along the same lines as we understand 'a metal' or 'a wine' as meaning 'a kind of . . . '; but even given this, an instance-of-fog has no more of a characteristic shape than does fog.

It is when we attempt to extend this descriptive principle to terms like 'paper', which appear at first sight to be counter-examples, that the connection with what are in effect judgements of essential properties becomes clear. The sense of 'shape' we are concerned with is not a purely perceptual one. It seems at first to be true that paper has a characteristic shape, roughly that of the thing you are now reading. However, it would be more accurate to say that what has a characteristic shape is a *sheet* of paper, not paper itself — we could imagine paper being milled into alternative shapes with no difficulty. The shape it usually has is an obvious consequence of its function, which imposes severe constraints on it. But paper itself no more has a characteristic shape than does ice-cream, even though ice-cream almost invariably comes in cones or blocks. It makes no sense to say of something that it has the shape of paper (contrast 'the feel of paper'). Characteristic shape means, then, 'a shape which is essential or necessary to' rather than 'a shape which is typically but contingently associated with'. So although there is a correlation between a linguistic property — being denoted by a mass term — and a property which is partly perceptual (shape is not an arbitrary concept for us but one which is directly linked to the nature of our perceptual system, presumably) nevertheless 'characteristic shape' goes beyond the purely perceptual and must make reference to other cognitive systems. We cannot tell what the characteristic shape of something is by looking at it, for we need to know how it would look under other circumstances.

In the same way that the syntactic category of countable nouns does not correspond entirely with the semantic notion of a nameable, as discussed earlier, so the category of mass noun does not coincide completely with the notion of what we might call 'substance'. Some distinctions emerge among the nouns which by syntactic criteria count as mass nouns if we examine Quine's (1960:90-1) semantic criterion for mass terms: for any mass term W, any collection of things which are W is itself W, or in the terms of our earlier metalanguage: if x and y both satisfy W, and the sum of x + y satisfies W, then W is a mass term. Put this way, both 'furniture' and 'water' are mass nouns. But if we turn the criterion around: for a mass term W, any subpart of W is itself W, a difference emerges. For both these examples this criterion is true only down to a certain level of detail: a chairleg is not an item of furniture and an atom of oxygen is not water. But above this level of detail it holds true: a chair is an item of furniture, and any non-atomic subpart of water is water. The difference is that subparts of furniture meeting the criterion are also regarded as nameables: chairs, tables, sofas, etc. But subparts of water are substances, not nameables. In the sense in which 'substance' is here understood, furniture is not substance, therefore.

It may be that an inclusive superordinate term like 'furniture' is treated linguistically as a mass term because there is actually no characteristic shape to be associated with it: it is difficult to imagine a furniture shape as opposed to a chair shape (Rosch *et al.* 1976), whereas for a countable superordinate term like 'animal' it might be just about possible to conceive of an 'animal shape'. Or it may be that there is a certain arbitrariness as to whether these terms are treated as countable or uncountable. It does not seem difficult to imagine that we might instead of 'furniture' have had a word 'furrutine' such that 'chair' and 'table' bear the same relation to it as 'dog' and 'cat' do to 'animal' and sentences like 'My house is filled with second-hand furrutines' or 'That chair is a fine furrutine' would be acceptable. But what is not arbitrary is that if someone invents a new substance which does not have a characteristic shape it will be described by a mass term and not by a count noun: 'plastic' and 'polythene' would be real life examples.

A further dimension relevant to whether something is describable by a mass term is what we might call 'collectivity'. If groups of similar (usually small) objects are typically encountered as a collection rather than as individual specimens they are likely to be designated by a mass term. Words for flowers and plants are good examples here: 'clover', 'mint' and 'wheat' are mass terms, 'dandelion', 'daisy' and 'nettle' are countable.[4] However, there is a great deal of cross-linguistic variation here and so to some extent the distinction must be arbitrary: e.g. Lyons (1968:282) points out that whereas in English 'grape' is countable and 'fruit' a mass noun, in German and Russian the reverse is true of 'grape' and in French and Russian the reverse is true of 'fruit'.

It might be objected, returning to the question of shape, that we have got the priority of events the wrong way round here: that we regard something as having no shape precisely because it is denoted by a mass term, and that this is a purely linguistic property connected to the semantic category of mass term. It is certainly true that if someone uses a mass term, we cannot make any linguistically based inference about its shape even though the actual referent might have a quite clear and characteristic shape: if someone says 'Have some chicken', offering a leg, for example. I think that the correct interpretation of this is that central instances of mass terms do not have a characteristic shape and that this is a fact about *them*, not a wholly linguistic fact. But this fact is also semantically associated with the linguistic category of 'mass term' such that by using a word which also occurs elsewhere as a count noun as a mass term it can be conveyed that the item in question does not have a salient shape, in much the same way that abstract events or processes can be reified by being denoted by a nominal. With mass terms, in most cases in fact, it is also conveyed that the item is a subpart of some larger entity, as with words for foods or materials or even objects ('I need some more table to spread my work out on').

V

Once given a world of nameables, the next task is to discover the principles by which they are grouped together into categories. Strictly speaking, this is an artificial distinction: we can already regard a nameable as a category with only one member: it makes no sense to talk about something being picked out *tout court*; we always mean that it has been picked out as a such-and-such. (In fact we could also say that there was a category of 'nameables'.) And any criterion that could pick out a nameable for the nonce could define a category by simply extending to other similar instances. Similarity always means similarity in a certain respect: the dimensions of similarity which seem most immediately relevant are those of appearance, behaviour and function, i.e. exactly those dimensions relevant to individuation in the first place.

In fact, as we shall see later, similarity as the basis for categorisation can be overruled by more sophisticated beliefs about the internal structure of the members, but for the most part it is the case that things fall into categories like cup, chair, finger, table, hand, cat, tree and hairbrush because, within a certain tolerance, they have certain properties in common. Let us call these categories 'basic' categories. Basic categories are also grouped together into higher order categories: chairs and tables are both members of the category 'furniture', cats and dogs are members of the category 'animal', all are members of the category 'physical object', and so on. At this level the basis for grouping certain objects together is not always so straightforward: the members of the category 'furniture' are not straightforwardly classified on the basis of shape or function, rather, some combination of both along with perhaps their typical location. It may be that all members of the category 'animal' share some aspect of their appearance together, but it is a fairly abstract aspect of their appearance if they do.

The implication of Quine's work, to return to an earlier theme, is that whenever we categorise an X as a Y, we are also assigning X to an implicit ontological category Z, like 'physical object', 'object stage' and so on. Quine's claim is that there are many different possible Zs all of which are 'right'. Now, it is obvious that at the level of explicit categorisation (explicit because we can, more or less, define the category extensionally, and we know its name ('rabbit', for example)) that of all the logically possible categorisations of the world which could be made, very few actually are made. No language, it is safe to assume, has a name for a category consisting of just teacups, treacle and loud noises, or similar heterogeneous collections of things. The answer given to Quine has asserted, in effect, that the same is true of implicit categories; of all the logically possible types of implicit categories available, very few are actually used — essentially, those which are implied by (N1)-(N4). This suggests that the line of enquiry to pursue is one which involves a further search for some principles which will distinguish the 'natural' *systems* of categories from the unnatural though possible systems of categories, whether they are implicit or explicit. Given that we only arrive at certain types of category, is it also the case that these categories are only *related* to each other in a certain type of fashion?

In order to approach this question, let us define, in the most deliberately general terms, a notion of a 'categorial framework'.[5] We can specify a categorial framework by specifying

(i) the categories and their members (which may of course be other categories);
(ii) the relationship or relationships existing between categories and their members.

For our purposes, a category can be seen as a collection of nameables or categories which are grouped together in some respect or other. When we speak of someone having or forming a category we mean that he has acquired some way of assigning things into a category.

The specification of a categorial framework in these terms by no means exhausts our interest in it since as yet no reference to linguistic properties has been made: there would be nothing in the preceding to prevent us from in principle hypothesising particular categorial frameworks for cats, say (if we thought they had concepts like nameable or even substance). But we will obviously want to know about the mapping of the vocabulary or sub-vocabularies of a natural language onto the categorial framework or frameworks which we can reasonably postulate to be attributable to the native speakers of that language. Conversely, language will be one major source of evidence for categorial frameworks: whereas particular nameables are denoted by proper names or demonstratives, the use of a general term can be taken, as suggested earlier, as evidence for the existence of a category to which all the nameables falling under that general term belong. Nevertheless, it still makes sense to ask whether all categories have names, for given other means of identifying categories the possibility arises that some may be entirely covert, describable only by some circumlocution like 'things which can be carried by an adult human'.[6] We will of course need some criterion for what counts as a name in this context, for we have already pointed out that there is a difference between being named and being merely describable. For example, the category 'physical object' by most criteria would not count as having a name, though 'physical object' clearly labels the category.

Now that we have introduced the notion of a categorial framework we can rephrase our original question about what principles are behind the grouping together of objects in a category as a slightly more specific question about the details of the relationships figuring in the second part of the definition of a framework: about the relation between members (nameables) of a category, and between categories and other categories.

It has already been said that the fact that an individual can be described by a general name like 'rabbit' is sufficient to enable us to infer that there is a corresponding category containing other similar individuals. More generally, judgements of entailment or of truth ('a chicken is a bird', 'if something is a chicken, then it is a bird') provide evidence for categories and their members. Clearly, if someone assents to both 'a robin is a bird' and 'a chicken is a bird' but not to 'a dog is a bird' then we are entitled to infer that he uses a category which contains chickens and robins but not dogs. Where such judgements are our main evidence, then the major principle relating members and categories can be reconstructed in terms of set membership or the 'is a' relationship: we will always be dealing with a partial taxonomy or what in the terms of Kay (1971) is called a 'taxonomic structure'.

A taxonomy of this sort is a categorial framework consisting of

(a) a (finite) set C of (non empty) categories
(b) a relation on C of proper inclusion such that (i) one category contains all the others and (ii) no member of a category can belong to more than one of its subcategories.

To describe such a structure a little more precisely we can add to our earlier metalanguage a stock of variables n, n', n" ... ranging over the objects picked out by (N1)-(N4), and c, c', c" ... ranging over categories (sets of nameables, and sets of categories) and a relation M (membership) between nameables and categories.[7] We also need a few other simple definitions:

76 Naïve metaphysics

$c = c'$ $= df\ (\forall n)\ (M(n, c) \leftrightarrow M(n, c'))$ (Identity of categories)

$DIS(c, c') = df\ \sim \exists n\ (M(n, c) \wedge M(n, c'))$ (Disjointness of categories)

$PI(c, c') = df\ (\forall n)\ (M(n, c') \rightarrow M(n, c) \wedge c \neq c')$

(c is properly included in c')

A taxonomic structure is a collection of categories such that for the relevant range of individuals:

$(\exists c)\ (\forall n)\ (M(n, c))$ (There is one all-inclusive category)

$(\forall n)\ (\forall c)\ (\forall c')\ (M(n, c) \wedge M(n, c') \leftrightarrow PI(c, c') \vee PI(c', c))$
(No individual in a category is in more than one of its subcategories at the same level)

We can display a categorial framework of such a type in an obvious way

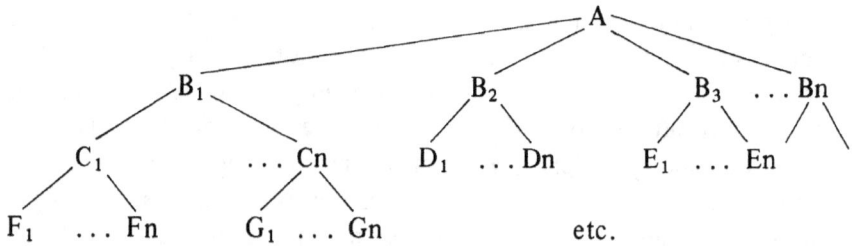

where A is the 'unique beginner' in Kay's terms, the all-inclusive category, and the elements at the bottom of the tree are what he calls the 'terminal elements', or the final partitioning of members of categories: for us they are nameables (or perhaps it would be more consistent to call them singletons containing a nameable).

Perhaps the simplest not obviously false hypothesis (though it *is* false) about the organisation of the lexical items of a natural language, given the existence of semantic relations like that between 'chicken' and 'bird' above, is that they map one-to-one onto a structure, or perhaps a set of structures of this sort. If we discount synonymy and polysemy which would be obvious exceptions to the one-one requirement, such a picture is what seems to be implied by many empiricist and 'abstractionist' accounts of category formation and the acquisition of word meaning, and to be quite widespread in the recent psychological literature (Fodor, Bever and Garrett 1974:205-7).

The classic source of such a view, and the clearest expression of it, is of course Locke's account in Book III of his *An Essay Concerning*

Human Understanding where he describes the acquisition of 'general names' in terms of the omission from 'particular ideas' of 'that which is peculiar to each' retaining 'only what is common to them all' (1964 edn: 265). Locke illustrates how the idea of 'man' might be arrived at from individual instances; how 'man' and 'horse' might be comprehended in 'animal'; how 'animal' might be seen to differ from other living things by omitting 'sense' and 'spontaneous motion', and so how

> by the same way the mind proceeds to body, substance, and at last to being, thing, and such universal terms which stand for any of our ideas whatsoever. (p. 266)

Thus categories are formed by the mind taking note of similarities existing in nature, and they will be arranged as a taxonomy, since each abstraction defines a category containing as members the individuals from which the abstraction has been made. At some points Locke also seems to imagine that all of the relevant vocabulary could be mapped onto a single taxonomy: at least, this seems to be what is implied by reference to a 'universal term' standing for any of our ideas whatsoever. But of course, given the existence of objects which belong to more than one category, where neither category includes the other — in other words, given the phenomenon of cross-classification — this cannot be the case.

There are some purely philosophical objections which can be made to Locke's account even if we were to sympathise with his general outline. The concept of abstraction that he proposes seems to be circular: given that logically any two things might be similar in any number of respects (being visible to the observer, weighing less than a whale, etc., etc.) in order to focus on the relevant similarity you would already have to have the concept being abstracted (Geach 1957:18). The alternative is to presuppose innate standards of similarity (as even Quine does) which are sufficient to narrow the range of alternatives down to where generalisation and discrimination can abstract properties, but then similarity alone is sufficient to do the job.

Unfortunately, even apart from the conceptual problems involved in abstractionist accounts of how such a taxonomy might arise, several rudimentary observations are sufficient to disprove successively weaker versions of the plausible sounding hypothesis with which we started, namely that all lexical relations can be explained by relating them to taxonomic structures. The fact that some categories, for example 'apple', can be members of more than one other category ('fruit' and 'food'), where these two are not related by proper inclusion (not all fruit is food, not all food is fruit) shows already that the vocabulary of English is not organised into a single overall taxonomy. It was in any case obvious to Locke that adjectives cross-classify nouns ('male' and 'female', 'edible' and 'inedible') but this example also shows that even if we restrict the hypothesis to mention of a single syntactic category like 'noun', there must still be more than one such taxonomy, these overlapping perhaps at various points. This second weaker hypothesis is also falsified as a complete description of lexical organisation by the existence of categorial frameworks in which categories are related by principles other than set membership or the 'is a' relation. We have already mentioned terms which designate wholes and parts: 'finger', 'hand', 'arm' and other words for parts of the body; 'branch' and 'tree' and so on. With some artificiality we can describe the various individuals designated by these terms as grouping into categories. As before, we can infer the relationship between the categories from judgements of truth and entailment: 'A finger is part of a hand', 'If it is a finger, then it is part of a hand'. Such statements are as firm as 'a chicken is a bird' or 'cats are animals' (Bever and Rosenbaum 1971). But for categorial frameworks such as this the relation of inclusion or 'is a' is not one both between nameables and categories, and between categories and categories, but one which holds just between nameables and categories — a particular individual can be said to be a member of a category 'finger', but the category 'finger' is not a member of the category 'hand', nor is a finger. Members of these categories are related to members of other categories by the relation 'part of' ('proper part of' in terms of the metalanguage employed earlier), not by M or by Proper Inclusion.

Let us consider for a while the hypothesis that 'is a' and 'part of' are the only relating principles we have to deal with. If it were the case that all semantic relations among nouns were of the types discussed then we could provide a straightforward and systematic account of the various semantic judgements that speakers are able to make concerning them. (We are assuming for the moment that these are semantic relations: see note 9.) Given a specification of the categories to which the individuals involved belong, and an indication of the relationships obtaining between categories and members, as well as a mapping of vocabulary onto the categories, we could define various semantic properties along the following lines (for a taxonomy):

(n, n' are nameables, c, c' are categories, N, N'; C, C' are their names)

(i) ⌜N is a C⌝ is true iff M(n, c)
(ii) ⌜A C is a C′⌝ is true iff PI (c, c′)
(iii) ⌜N is a C⌝ entails ⌜N is a C′⌝ iff M(n, c) and PI(c,c′)
— and so on.

For a part-whole framework the semantic properties are obviously different, as are the properties of the framework: such a structure is a collection of categories such that for the relevant range of individuals:

(iv) $(\exists c)(\forall n)(\exists n')(PP(n, n') \wedge M(n', c))$

i.e. there is some category consisting of the 'whole' nameables of which all the other nameables are parts, and:

(v) $(\forall c)(\forall c')(\forall n)(\forall n')(M(n, c) \wedge M(n', c') \wedge PP(n, n') \leftrightarrow DIS(c, c'))$

i.e. the categories containing these proper parts are not related to each other by inclusion.

The semantic properties are simply as follows (as before, N, N′, etc., are the names of n, n′):

(vi) ⌜N is part of N′⌝ is true iff PP(n, n′)
(vii) ⌜A C is part of a C′⌝ (or ⌜A C′ has a C⌝) is true iff
    $(\forall n)(\forall n')(M(n, c) \wedge M(n', c') \rightarrow PP(n, n'))$

Thus we can define in a fairly rigorous fashion the semantic relationships implied by that mapping of a vocabulary onto categorial frameworks of this sort.[8]

One attraction of such a procedure is that it looks like the sort of thing which, together with an appropriate combinatorial mechanism of the type discussed at the beginning of the chapter, would allow us coverage of a wide variety of valid inferences for a language, a traditional requirement on theories of meaning. Of course, this is a result that can be achieved in many other ways: meaning postulates, for example. If we were able to identify the categories independently of any semantic judgements then this procedure would in fact be preferable on at least one score to using meaning postulates, for we could then reduce semantic judgements to other facts. But if we use semantic judgements in setting up the categorial frameworks then in using the frameworks to describe semantic properties we are indulging in an exercise which is just as circular and non-explanatory as the inclusion of meaning postulates in semantic description. Even so, there is some other advantage to categorial frameworks here, for they reveal more clearly the interrelations between words which are only implicit in a list of meaning postulates. Furthermore, this method does not claim that the relation between the words in question is analyticity, whereas on the usual construal of them, meaning postulates do. What is most attractive about the procedure, however, is that it enables us to give a reasonably plausible and fairly tight reconstruction of what might be meant by the Quinean claim that, logical truths aside, sentences involving semantic connections between words are not thereby absolutely true or false, but only true or false with respect to the system of beliefs in which they are embedded. Changing a sufficient number of such beliefs could change the truth value of some of these sentences, and alter the pattern of valid entailments. Thus with respect to the categorial framework in which the categories named by 'bat' and 'owl' are both properly included in the category named by 'bird', then both the statements 'an owl is a bird' and 'a bat is a bird' (alternatively, the entailments 'if something is an owl, it is a bird' and 'if something is a bat, it is a bird') will be judged to be true. The categorial framework with which the majority of English speakers operate, however, disallows the inference 'a bat is a bird' since the category 'bird' does not include 'bat'. Having once isolated a particular categorial framework, by whatever means, then we are able to describe different mappings of vocabulary onto it, and mappings of one vocabulary onto different categorial frameworks, in a way which seems in some important respects to correspond to the notion 'true with respect to some system of beliefs'.[9]

There is another possibility which arises from a choice of this method of semantic description. Given an independent account of what it is that makes us group some set of objects into a category — some psychological account of the principles constitutive of category membership, then we could approach not just a description of semantic relationships like those detailed above, but, to the extent that they could be related to non-linguistic facts about our cognitive abilities, an explanation for them. This explanation would have the form: ⌜As are Bs⌝ is true (with respect to this sytem of beliefs) because everything that is a member A is also a member of B. This in turn is because...'where the independent account of category formation and membership supplies the remainder. We do not have any such account as yet, though some candidates will be examined later, but this pattern of explanation seems a little more promising and certainly more satisfying than the type which runs: ⌜As are Bs⌝ is true because there is a meaning postulate to the effect that all As are Bs', or the type of explanation which says that: ⌜As are Bs⌝ is true because all the markers to be found in the semantic representation of B are also to be found in the representation of A'.

However, it is clear that if this pattern of explanation proves to be feasible at all, it will be valid for only a small set of the semantic judgements that people can make. As well as the obvious objections (a) that we have not dealt with less tangible or abstract entities ('nightmares are dreams'), or with examples which seem to be genuinely analytic or to do with definitions, (b) that it is not easy to give a treatment in similar terms of other syntactic categories like verbs, adverbs or adjectives, there is the fact (c) that there are other semantic relations between nouns which describe physical objects, which seem to resist such an approach. For example, there is the relation which we might label 'consists of' or 'contains' which holds between 'army' and 'soldier' and between 'wood' (in its countable sense) and 'tree'. It is presumably just as firmly true that a wood contains trees, and that an army contains soldiers as that cats are animals, or that fingers are parts of hands. There is even in fact some evidence that this relation is more 'natural', in the sense that it is ontogenetically prior to the relation of membership (Markman, Horton and McLanahan 1980).

But what is the relation between the category of woods and the category of trees? Not all members of the category of trees are members of the category of woods. Do we want to identify a wood with the set of trees it consists of? Commonsense and the dictionary would suggest that woods can also contain bushes and various other sorts of undergrowth or even clearings which we would still say were part of the wood. To equate a wood with a set of trees seems unbearably artificial. If we defined a scattered wood-individual (that unique individual such that it is discrete from everything that is discrete from a wood, a vice versa) consisting of the sum of all individual woods, and a scattered tree-individual in the same way, then the two individuals would overlap. But neither is contained in the other and 'overlap' is too general a notion to derive the semantic properties needed.

Consider too the relation between 'army' and 'soldier'. Does the set of all soldiers contain the same individuals as the set of all armies? Or can a soldier not belong to an army? Our intuitions are just not very clear about this: all we can be sure of is that neither of these examples will yield comfortably to a description in terms of M or O.

So we can abandon any hope of completeness even concerning

nouns describing physical objects. But we can still hope to explore in more detail the principles by which categories are formed and by which members and categories are related, for it seems clear that these will form an important component of any overall attempt at explaining the basis for at least some semantic judgements.

Notes

1. This is so if we mean 'language' literally. But it might make sense to ask about some animals whether they have a system of internal representation of objects, within which some objects can be regarded as single or unique in some way. Perhaps we would allow that, if so, such animals had a notion of 'nameable' comparable to our own.

2. The term 'naïve physics' is from Hayes (1978).

3. As well as SUM (x, y) we defined $PR(x, y)$ — the common part of two overlapping individuals. In the case where x and y are nameables, I have not been able to discover any candidates for named products, or even any examples of products not covered by P or PP.

4. I am grateful to Jim Hurford for these examples.

5. This traditional term is used in a rather different context in Korner (1970), from whom I originally obtained it.

6. See Berlin, Breedlove and Raven (1968) and Basso (1968) for some interesting discussion of such categories and the problem of identifying them, with reference to languages with 'classifier' systems.

7. Clearly we no longer have a purely nominalistic metalanguage if we do this, but that is of no concern for our purposes.

8. It follows from these definitions that from 'A is part of B' and 'B is part of C' we can infer that 'A is part of C'. While if the actual objects bear the relation 'PP' this will technically be true, it may not always be appropriate. See Bever and Rosenbaum (1971:591,fn.b) and Cruse (1979) for examples and discussion.

9. This being the case, it might perhaps be thought inappropriate to call the relations in question semantic rather than pragmatic, since essentially we are attributing to speakers a particular set of beliefs about the world, and a mapping of vocabulary onto that conceptual structure. We will go on later to the claim that there is a difference between the kind of judgement of necessary truth (in a sense of 'necessary' to be dealt with in Chapter 6) involved here and those which might more properly be called analytic. Those concerned with categorial frameworks are necessary only with respect to that framework, and that framework depends to a large extent on the way the world is or the way it is believed to be. The latter type, on the other hand, are more dependent on linguistic facts. But in their different ways, both can be called 'semantic' judgements.

4   THEORIES OF CATEGORISATION

I

There is a recent tradition of work in anthropology and in psychology which can be interpreted as providing both evidence about the relationships between categories grouped into frameworks, and as an attempt at explaining the principles governing the grouping of individuals into categories. From this work it emerges that in some areas of vocabulary at least the hypothesis that the corresponding categorial frameworks are a series of possibly overlapping taxonomic structures is correct, at least in outline. Furthermore, there seem to be some interesting universally shared properties belonging to these taxonomic structures which may give a clue to the principles underlying their formation.

Berlin and his associates (1973, summarised in Berlin 1978) have examined a number of such structures, based on the vocabulary of folk-biology from a wide range of sources and suggest tentatively that they consist universally of no more than five, occasionally six classes of categories (taxa, in their terminology). At the highest level (0) is the 'unique beginner', or 'kingdom', which in many languages, they say, is 'not labelled linguistically by a single habitual expression'. They are categories representing the broadest division of the natural world. In English 'plant' and 'animal' are such names. At the next level (1) occur 'life form' categories, which only appear at this level. Examples in English would be 'tree', 'flower', 'vegetable'. They are typically few in number (Berlin *et al.* quote 5-10), are never terminal (i.e. they always include other categories) and are generally named by what they call 'primary lexemes'. Primary lexemes are either monolexemic items — not further analysable — or composite forms which are not in contrast with other forms containing one or more of the same lexemes. For example, 'horse chestnut' and 'sweet chestnut' are in a 'contrast set': they subdivide the category 'chestnut'. They are thus secondary lexemes. But 'monkey-puzzle tree', though not monolexemic, does not contrast with anything — there are no 'cow-puzzle' or 'fox-puzzle' trees. Thus it counts as a primary lexeme.

The most numerous categories are 'generic' at level (2). They are named by primary lexemes and are the most commonly referred to groupings of organisms in natural environment, are the most salient psychologically and are likely to be among the first taxa learnt by the child. (1973:216)

Examples from English are claimed to be 'oak', 'willow' and 'pine', etc., but as we shall see, this may not be so. Usually generic categories appear at level (2) but occasionally at level (1) (i.e. they are not included in a life form category), especially when the category in question is of particular economic importance, or is distinctive in some way. 'Cactus' would be an example of the latter in English, and this example suggests that it is perhaps the fact that they are difficult to classify along with more widespread types of plant that can cause them to appear at level (1).

At levels (3) and (4) (unless included in a generic at level (1)) come 'specific' and 'varietal' categories. They are few in number, occur in contrast sets, and are named by secondary lexemes. They are terminal or include categories which are designated by secondary lexemes. Examples of specific categories in English are 'weeping willow', 'dwarf willow' and 'white willow'. If there were such things as (say) 'straight-leaved dwarf willow' and 'curly-leaved dwarf willow', these would be varietal categories.

We can summarise all of this in an obvious fashion:

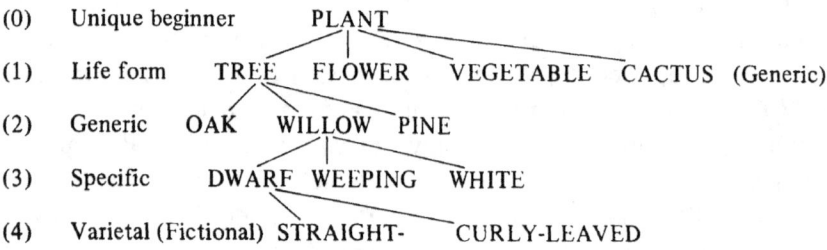

Level

(0) Unique beginner   PLANT
(1) Life form   TREE   FLOWER   VEGETABLE   CACTUS   (Generic)
(2) Generic   OAK   WILLOW   PINE
(3) Specific   DWARF WEEPING WHITE
(4) Varietal (Fictional) STRAIGHT-   CURLY-LEAVED

Berlin *et al.* also claim that in many languages there may be intermediate covert (i.e. unlabelled) categories, the existence of which can be demonstrated in various ways. The kind of experimental techniques employed here (not only by Berlin and his associates: see also Anglin (1977), Miller (1971)) are various but the following is typical of the kind of test which is often used. First, a group of speakers are instructed to sort a group of words or objects into, say, three classes, either on some completely unspecified intuitive basis, or specified rather vaguely 'those you feel belong together'. Suppose that with significant agreement they do so, giving us classes A, B and C. Then a further group (or the same group) are invited to class the same words or objects into, say, two groups: again with significant agreement they produce D and E. Obviously, even if they cannot describe explicitly the basis for their second classification decision, if it should turn out that D = A and E = B+C then we would be entitled to infer that B and C belong in some higher level category, even if this category does not have a name, and even if they do not exhaust the contents of this category.

In this area of folk-biology then, the categorial frameworks which can be postulated have largely predictable properties: they are taxonomic hierarchies with possibly unlabelled all-inclusive categories and one level (the generic) which contains proportionately many more members than other levels. Roughly the same thing appears to be true in fact for categorial frameworks where the members are related by 'part of', in so far as these have been examined in any detail. For example, Anderson (1978:348) reports that body-part hierarchies rarely exceed a depth of five or six, just as for taxonomic structures.

Obviously these findings call out for an explanation. Why should we find structures having these properties and not others? In gross terms, of course, there is presumably no great mystery about this. Generic categories seem to correspond to the basic level of categorisation at which different kinds of chairs, dogs and hairbrushes are grouped together: as individuals they are perceptually and functionally distinct from other objects, and there is a high degree of similarity between individuals. As Berlin puts it (1978:19), somewhat unhelpfully, generic categories are formed 'because they are there'. They reflect the most economical cutting up of the environment. Categorisations at a finer level, taking account of more detailed differences between objects, are presumably a response to culturally or socially important discriminations: specific and varietal categories are formed 'because it is culturally important to do so'. What about the higher level categories? We might advance the speculation that categorisation at a coarser, more inclusive level might represent in part the beginnings of folk-science (and real science), where objects are classified together perhaps at first merely on the basis of perceptual similarities, but later upon the basis of some tacit hypothesis that the objects have something in common over and above their easily observable similarities, or even despite some easily observable dissimilarities. This tacit hypothesis might turn out to be wrong when made explicit, but finding out that it is wrong is the beginning of forms of scientific enquiry.

II

Although an explanation for the properties of these systems of categorisation in terms of 'usefulness' or 'maximisation of information' or 'in response to cultural pressure' may be intuitively correct and even rather obvious, it is maddeningly vague. But it is important to search for some way of putting such a hypothesis to the test, in order both to add some flesh to the explanation, and more crucially, because it is notoriously the case that hypotheses which seem obviously true when formulated at such a level of generality can turn out to be quite false when investigated more closely.

An interesting series of papers by Rosch and her associates (Rosch 1973, Rosch and Mervis 1975, Rosch et al. 1976, summarised in Rosch 1978), can be seen as an attempt to do just this — to provide and test exactly this fuller account of 'cognitive or cultural usefulness', as well as providing some further interesting findings concerning the exact relationship between a category and its members. In research reported in 1973, Rosch showed that speakers could make consistent judgements about the degree of membership of an item in a category; about how good an example of a category a particular instance was. For example, there was significant agreement on the following rankings of categories and their members, where the head of the list represents the best example, the last, the worst:

Fruit: apple, plum, pineapple, strawberry, fig, olive.
        (an apple is a better example of fruit than an olive)
Vehicle: car, boat, scooter, tricycle, horse, skis.
        (a car makes a better vehicle than a scooter)

These rankings correlated significantly with the frequencies of response of an item as an example of a category (Battig and Montague 1969) — where a subject is asked for an example of 'fruit' he is more likely to say 'apple' than 'olive'. However, the rankings did not correlate with judgements of preference for the items named — the fact that you may like pineapples more than apples does not affect your judgement that apples are better examples of 'fruit'. Furthermore, judgements of the truth of central sentences ('an apple is a fruit') were significantly faster than judgements for peripheral sentences ('an olive is a fruit') for both adults and children, suggesting that whatever procedure checks statements of category membership for their truth operates more effectively on good examples than on bad examples. Children, though, made more errors on peripheral sentences, suggesting that central instances of categories ('apple') might be learned first. Rosch calls these central instances 'prototypes' of the category.

This demonstration that categories have 'internal structure', as Rosch puts it, is significant in many respects. First, it is sufficient to demonstrate the psychological implausibility of a simple model of word-meaning which sees the meaning of a word like 'fruit' as the conjunction of a series of properties, each and every one of which must be possessed by an item in order for it to be a member of the category in question — or, in other words, that there are necessary and sufficient conditions for being a fruit. If this were the case then any kind of task involving positive judgements of membership in a category should produce the same results for all the members of the category, since in each case what is going on is the 'checking off' of a list of criterial features. No doubt different assumptions about the checking off process could make the model consistent with these findings, but without them these findings are sufficient to refute the naïve psychological analogue of a componential theory in which the meaning of a word like 'fruit' is completely given by an enumeration of the primitives of which it is composed.

Secondly, these results demonstrate that the natural interpretation, in terms of taxonomic structures, of the relation between a category and its members: that all the members are 'equidistant' from the category which includes them, is incorrect. Rather, some members of the category are central, or nearer to the category itself. In other words, to say simply that the relationship is one of proper inclusion, is, while true, not sufficiently explicit, for it does not take into account the fact that the category is structured, if Rosch is correct, as a prototype or central instance with less central instances grouped around it accordingly. (This is true at least for the relation between life form and generic categories and their non-biological equivalents, which are the ones tested in this experiment.)

Finally, the results suggest a reason why taxonomic structures, and the associated relations between categories and their members, should have the features that they do. Rosch suggests that it is possible that

> cultures come to define as best examples of categories those members which are maximally different from other categories on the same level of linguistic contrast. Such a principle would render categories maximally discriminable, and suggests a specific cognitive mechanism underlying the evolution of internal structure. Maximum

88 *Theories of categorisation*

> discriminability would also result if best examples of categories were those instances which were not also salient members in other categories... (p. 143)

If categories are formed so as to exploit perceptual, functional or behavioural differences to the full, the best examples in a category would be those which either did not figure at all in other categories, or were not salient in other categories which are at the same level of contrast. Furthermore, the level at which perceptual or functional differences are most marked should also be the level at which there will be, relatively speaking, a proliferation of categories: these differences will cry out to be taken advantage of in the evolving system of categorisation.

This possible influence of the tendency to maximum discriminability upon the formation of categories was explored further by Rosch *et al.* (1976). 'Maximum discriminability', with some oversimplification, can be associated with degree of 'cue validity', that is, the likelihood that a particular cue — some property or attribute of an object — signals the presence of a particular category rather than some other. 'Cue validity' is a term most easily construed as concerning perception, and it originates from work on pattern recognition (Reed 1978). However, it can be defined in various ways: in Rosch and Mervis (1975) it is defined for attributes of all types, not only perceptual, as

> the frequency of a cue being associated with the category in question divided by the total frequency of that cue over all relevant categories. (p. 575)

Thus for example 'having feathers' would be a cue having high validity for the category 'bird', since all (?) birds have feathers, and nothing which is not a bird (trout lures and chorus girls aside) has feathers. But 'having legs' would not be a cue of very high validity for 'bird' since birds, animals, men, insects and even tables all share this property. Cue validity for an entire category is the sum of the cue validities for each of its attributes. Obviously it is then possible that some categories, seen as collections of attributes, might have higher cue validities than others. This could be regarded as a reconstruction of the notion of some categories having a greater information content than others, and this is Rosch's intention.

Rosch *et al.* (1976) present evidence that:

categories within taxonomies of concrete objects are structured such that there is generally one level of abstraction at which the most basic category cuts can be made. In general, the basic level of abstraction in a taxonomy is the level at which categories carry the most information, possess the highest cue validity, and are, thus, the most differentiated from one another. (p. 383)

They suggest that such taxonomies are always organised such that there is a superordinate category ('animal') at the most inclusive level, above the basic level ('dog', 'cat') which in turn includes subordinate level categories ('spaniel', 'collie', 'siamese', 'tabby'). Their evidence for the claim that the basic level is the most informative comes from the listing of attributes for categories at each level obtained from subjects in experiments they describe. Given the way that cue validity is defined, categories having a large number of common attributes will always have a higher cue validity than those with a small number, provided that both sets of attributes are distributed with roughly equal frequency over other categories. Representative figures for the average number of attributes in common to categories at these three levels are as follows (adapted from p. 391):

	Superordinate	Basic	Subordinate
Fruit	3	8.3	9.5
Vehicle	1	11.7	16.8

It is the difference between the above scores which is significant, of course, since 'apple' obviously inherits all the attributes judged common to 'fruit' and so on. These results show that instances of the category 'fruit' are seen as having few attributes in common, of the category 'apple', 'pear', etc., quite a few attributes are shared, and of the subordinate category ('eating apple', etc.), not many more than they have inherited by virtue of their membership in the previous categories. So in terms of the attributes which subjects can discriminate as being characteristic of members of the various categories, the original intuition that the basic or generic level of categorisation is the most informative seems to be well confirmed. Basic level categories have higher cue validity than either superordinate or subordinate categories because superordinate categories have few common attributes, and the attributes of subordinate categories are mostly shared by the other subordinates of that basic category and hence do not contribute so heavily to total cue validity.

Further experiments showed that basic level objects are those for which something like an average shape can be identified – a prototypical apple can be visualised more easily than a prototypical fruit. And identification of pictures in 'visual noise' is aided if the subject is 'primed' with the basic level name (i.e. presented with it shortly before the recognition task), though performance is actually hindered by similar priming with superordinate names. Both of these findings suggest confirmation of the intuition that basic objects are more 'imageable'. Unfortunately, there is no information in Rosch's report of these findings as to a difference in imageability between superordinates like 'bird' and those like 'furniture', i.e. between count and mass nouns, though we might expect to find this, given the discussion of section IV, Chapter 3. Finally, Berlin et al.'s suggestion that basic level categories are those likely to be learned first by the child is supported by the fact that children can sort objects into basic level categories perfectly well right from the earliest period, though sorting into superordinate categories improves with age. This demonstrates that basic level categories are ontogenetically prior, and it has already been suggested by the earlier experiments that children acquire the names of these basic level categories first.

However, in one major respect the findings of Rosch differed significantly from those of Berlin. For although she demonstrated that the structural properties of biological taxonomies also hold of taxonomies of the domestic and man-made environment, in so far as one level is salient in many ways, the biological taxonomies she investigated – 'tree', 'fish' and 'bird' – did not behave as expected. It was hypothesised that, for example, 'tree' was the superordinate category and that 'oak', 'pine', 'willow', etc. would be the basic level objects: this would be in accordance with Berlin's findings. However, the number of attributes in common to the category 'tree' were 10, whereas to 'oak', etc. approximately 11 (p. 391). Thus it appears that it is 'tree' (and 'fish' and 'bird') which is the basic level category, at least for Rosch's subjects.

Rosch summarises the basis for the formation of categories as the outcome of two principles: (i) the principle of 'cognitive economy' (1978:28) which states that categories will form so as to be maximally informative: cue validity would be maximised. Clearly such a principle, if untrammelled, would lead to a proliferation of tiny categories, each individuated on the basis of a single unique attribute, for such an attribute, and hence such a category would then have the highest possible cue validity. However, principle (i) is constrained by (ii) the principle of 'perceived world structure' (p. 29) which states that as far as humans are concerned, the perceived world is not made up of random scatterings or clusterings of attributes, but that attributes will reliably co-occur in particular bundles. As Rosch puts it:

> given a knower who perceives the complex attributes of feathers, fur, and wings, it is an empirical fact provided by the perceived world that wings co-occur with feathers more than with fur. And given an actor with motor programmes for sitting, it is a fact of the perceived world that objects with the perceptual attributes of chairs are more likely to have functional sit-on-ableness than objects with the appearance of cats (1978:29)

So some particular bundles of attributes will have a higher composite cue validity than any random collection of attributes, and a category formed around these attributes will be correspondingly more informative than some logically possible category consisting of attributes which do not always occur together. This, roughly speaking, is Rosch's explanation for why we do not have a category consisting solely of teacups, treacle and loud noises: the attributes of 'teacups' would have low cue validity for that category since they are present in many other categories; 'treacle' likewise shares properties with other categories, and though 'loud noises' share no properties with anything else very much their attributes would contribute no more to the composite cue validity of this artificial category than they would to a category containing just loud noises.

However, Rosch does not restrict the principles of cognitive economy to the formation of categories. In Rosch and Mervis (1975) it is also suggested that within categories (of any level) the pressure of maximisation of discriminability governs the formation of the internal structure of categories: prototypes and groupings around prototypes. The crucial notion to which she makes appeal here is that of 'family resemblance' within a category. Wittgenstein (1972: sections 66, 67) as is well known, argued that theories of word meaning or definition involving necessary and sufficient conditions were inappropriate for many words. His example was 'game': there are few properties, if any, shared by all games. Rather, he argued, one game shares features with the next, and that shares some features (not necessarily the same ones) with the next one, and so on. The point is that some pairs of games might not share any features with each other, though they would share at least one feature with one other game. The point can be illustrated with an artificial example:

ABC   BCD   CDE   DEF   EFG   FGH

There is no one letter in common to all of this series and several members share no letter at all, but each shares two letters with its neighbour.

Rosch defines a measure of family resemblance which is similar to that of cue validity described earlier. Given the members of a category and the attributes (derived again from listings by subjects) of the members, each attribute can be given a number : the number of members of the category which possess the attribute. Then for each member the degree of family resemblance is the total of the numbers associated with its attributes. In other words, the higher the degree of family resemblance, the greater the number of attributes shared with other members of the category. The hypothesis to be tested was that the judgements of prototypicality obtained in earlier experiments ('a sparrow is a better example of a bird than a penguin') would correlate with the degree of family resemblance of the item in question. Prototype members of categories would be those which (a) shared most properties with other members of the category; (b) shared fewest properties with members of contrasting categories.

This was discovered to be the case for both superordinate and basic level categories. A prototypical member of the category 'furniture', say 'chair', shares most attributes with other members of the category ('table', etc.) and fewest with members of other categories at the same level ('tools', 'vehicles'). A prototypical type of 'chair' shares more features with other types of chair, and fewest with other subtypes of 'table'. For example, it is easy to imagine an object which is a high, hard, flat chair – not a central instance of 'chair' – which in fact possesses many of the attributes of 'table'. An armchair – a more central member of the category 'chair' – possesses fewer of the attributes of 'table'.

Rosch also suggests an explanation for the common feeling that there must be some features shared by all items of 'furniture' – some features which are defining characteristics of this category. What Rosch's results show is that this is in fact the case for the prototypes of the category : they do indeed share some central core of features. She suggests that these features are associated with the category name even though something might not possess them and yet still be a member of the category, thus accounting for this common but apparently wrong intuition. (Something can still be a member of the category by overlapping another of the features of a prototype.)

Summarising, Rosch states

> prototypes appear to be just those members of the category which most reflect the redundancy structure of the category as a whole. That is, categories form to maximise the information rich clusters of attributes in the environment and, thus, the cue validity of the attributes of categories; when prototypes of categories form by means of the principle of family resemblance, they maximise such clusters and such cue validity still further within categories. (p. 602)

Discriminable attributes do not cluster together randomly in the environment : something with feathers is also likely to have wings. Categories are formed reflecting these correlations : once something is judged to be in the category a large number of its attributes are thereby predictable. Within the category, some members share more of these attributes with their fellows than do other members. They are judged prototypical of the category in so far as more of the total number of attributes distributed among the members of the category are predictable from them (possessed by them) than from any other member. Thus both the salience of the basic level in a taxonomic structure, and the salience of prototypes within categories at all levels can be explained by a simple principle to the effect that categories form so as to maximise cue validity.

III

Before turning to some critical discussion of Rosch's work, it is worth pointing out that if her explanation of category formation is correct, then it provides us with another argument against the claimed indeterminacy of the ontological categories that we tacitly ascribe to the speakers of a language. As we saw earlier, Quine argues that we have no logical warrant to attribute to the speaker of another language a particular ontological category since some other category coextensive as far as available evidence goes, is always a possibility. We have no more right, for example, to translate 'gavagai' by 'rabbit' than by 'it is rabbiting'.

Quine could actually be construed as intending to suggest either of two things with this example of an exotic translation : either that his natives bracket together manifestations of rabbit along with manifestations of rain, snow and hail, i.e. they do not distinguish the concepts of (nameable) physical object and 'local weather'; or that their concept of 'rabbit' corresponds to our concept of local, temporary, weather conditions, leaving it open as to whether they also distinguish something corresponding to our physical object. But on either construal of Quine's translation, given the assumption of similarity of perceptual apparatus in our natives, and the correctness of Rosch's theory, the situation he envisages could not arise. Physical objects, for example, share properties like mass, extension, detachability from surroundings, permanence relative to members of other categories and so on. These properties regularly co-occur and we can form a category around them. It is true that it is possible that for other creatures other properties might be salient in physical objects and that a preponderance of these properties might also be found in temporary features of the environment like climatic conditions. On the assumption that these creatures also form categories which maximise regularities, then it is likely that they would form a category including both: hence 'it is rabbiting' (along with 'it is snowing', etc.) would be an accurate rendering. But this is only true *if* they are sensitive to different properties: if they are not, as we — and Quine — are assuming, then they would, if forming categories along the same principles, form the same categories as us. The same is true on the alternative construal of Quine: coextensive categories, given our assumptions, will be the same categories, for they will have been formed for the same reason: maximisation of the validity of the same perceptual cues, maximisation of what Rosch calls the 'redundancy structure' of the environment. Thus the hypothetical counter-argument which was raised when discussing experimental findings concerning the acquisition of the concept of 'physical object' by children (namely that even granting the various perceptual discriminations that were acquired, there is still no guarantee that they would lead to this concept), is not an argument that can be maintained.

Thus given any two categories which contain the same members, provided they are grouped together mostly on perceptual grounds, we can be sure that they are the same category. What we still have no guaranteed means of justifying, however, is the psychological description of the category in which the objects are included: we are perfectly justified in translating names of members by the name of the corresponding category in another language, but we have no certain way of knowing how to describe correctly the ontological category we are thereby ascribing to the speaker. But this only means that our descriptions of them must be hypotheses, to be tested and amended just like any other hypotheses.

In the case where the categories are observably not coextensive, then we do not have any logical justification for a translation along those lines. But this is exactly the case when, in real life, we are uncertain as to how to translate something. We are not sure whether to translate 'rug' into French as 'tapis' (see Lyons 1977) because there are some things a Frenchman would call a 'tapis' that we would not happily call a 'rug'. But we are happy to translate 'lapin' as 'rabbit' because the principles of category formation guarantee that if the categories are coextensive, they have been formed in response to the same clustering of attributes. As before, we might not know what to call the ontological category we are tacitly ascribing to the Frenchman, nor even that with which we are operating, but we are justified in assuming that they are the same.

It might be replied that because this argument depends on the assumption that perceptual mechanisms are constant for speakers of different languages, the demonstration of equivalence of categories can only be justified for categories determined entirely on perceptual criteria. It would not be true, for example, for categories defined wholly or partly in terms of functional and/or cultural criteria.

As far as the examples suggested by Quine are concerned, he seems in fact to assume that their definition is wholly in terms of perceptual criteria. And surely categories like physical object are virtually independent of functional and cultural considerations, in the sense that they are not culture relative, even though they may not be definable solely in terms of perceptual criteria, if 'perceptual' is construed narrowly as concerning purely instantaneous phenomenal features; since as we saw, memory must play some part. As regards cases which clearly are examples of functionally or culturally defined categories (an example like 'table' or 'marriage') the situation seems to be that the more closely the functional or cultural attributes constitutive of the category can be identified across languages or cultures, the more confident we are of the translation. For example, we might identify something (tentatively) as referring to a 'table' on grounds of the shape and location of its referents, but if it subsequently transpires that they are also used for sitting and sleeping on we would be cautious in translating the word in this way. In general, this sort of confidence seems to extend to only the most fundamental aspects of human social and personal activity: moving, eating, sleeping, excreting and reproducing. Beyond that — or even within it — cultural preoccupations determine what is to count as a salient attribute, though the principles of category formation are, we assume, the same once given these attributes. Translation, if this is correct, is not — between humans at any rate — indeterminate so much as extremely difficult.

After completing the original version of this section I was astonished to find in Quine's 'Natural Kinds' (1970) an account of category formation which amounts to a concession to the kind of argument just presented.[1] I had thought that a Quinean response to the argument might object to at least two points: the *a priori* assumption of perceptual similarity across the species, and (in view of the remarks in Quine 1971) appeal to psychological hypotheses in philosophical argument: i.e. the assumption that Rosch is more or less correct. But in Quine's account of the learning of natural kind terms in terms of ostension and induction and an innate 'quality space', he makes clear that he regards human perceptual apparatus and standards of similarity to be identical everywhere, and therefore to ensure that people presented with similar instances will form the same concept:

> At any rate, this is so if as seems plausible, each man's spacing of qualities is enough like his neighbor's . . . The uniformity of people's quality spaces virtually assures that similar presentations will elicit similar verdicts . . . (p. 164)

Nor is psychological evidence out of place in philosophical argument:

> There is no external vantage point, no first philosophy. All scientific findings, all scientific conjectures that are at present plausible, are therefore in my view as welcome for use in philosophy as elsewhere. (p. 165)

It is somewhat ironic that the psychological evidence in question is in any case of the kind that should be thoroughly amenable to even the most fervent behaviourist, since it assumes nothing beyond a tendency, presumably the result of evolution, for maximum efficiency in the category formation processes of human beings.

IV

While Rosch's account of the principles of category and prototype formation is the most comprehensive yet advanced, and apparently supported by a weight of experimental evidence, there are some aspects of it which are not beyond criticism. The exact status of prototypes in a theory of concepts or of word meaning is by no means clear, as we will see later, and her account of category formation is also problematic. Rosch herself (1978:41) points out that some of her assumptions about the nature of attributes are particularly difficult to justify. For example, it was assumed that the attributes upon which cue validities are computed were in some sense perceptual or functional givens, objectively identifiable in the real world independently of the category to which they belong. But when the attributes which were elicited from subjects are examined carefully, it becomes apparent that this is not so: what counts as a leg, for example, is very different for a man, a bird, a table and an insect. And a functional attribute like 'sit-on-able-ness' or 'seat' is something which seems to require prior recognition of the object as falling into the category 'chair': if only physical properties were involved then tables, rocks or packing cases are just as sit-on-able as chairs. Finally, many of the attributes offered by subjects were inherently relational, like 'large'; these also must involve prior assignment of the object to a category in order to determine the parameters for that particular property: what counts as large for a bird is not usually large for an animal.

The fact that many attributes are not identifiable prior to or independently of recognition of the category they belong to is an extremely damaging one for Rosch's theory. Although she attempts to minimise the damage by various arguments, they are not wholly successful. We can distinguish three separate arguments. First, she argues that she is presenting a 'structural hypothesis', a set of abstract formal principles of category formation not tied to any particular processing models or claims (1978:28). Secondly, that 'when we speak of the formation of categories, we mean their formation in the culture' (*op. cit.*) rather than in the individual; and finally, that the process by which attributes are individuated is in any case the same as the process by which basic categories are formed:

> the same laws of cognitive economy leading to the push toward basic level categories and prototypes might also lead to the definition of attributes of categories such that the categories once given would appear maximally distinctive from one another and such that the more prototypical items would appear even more representative of their own and less representative of contrastive categories. Actually, in the evolution of the meaning of terms in languages, probably both the constraint of real world factors and the construction and reconstruction of attributes are continually present. Thus, given a particular category system, attributes are defined such as to make the system appear as logical and economical as possible. (1978:42)

98 *Theories of categorisation*

This third argument, that attributes are formed in the same way as categories, concedes what was disguised by the choice of terminology: that attributes are themselves categories, either labelled in already existing vocabulary, like 'wings', 'legs' or 'feathers', or by rather more complex phrases like 'sit-on-able-ness'. The first two arguments on the other hand are intended to defuse any attempt to construe the principles as either a theory of category recognition, or a theory of category formation in the individual. For although the concept of cue validity originates from work on pattern recognition, and hence is naturally suited to such a role, it is clear that any attempt to advance a processing model of category recognition which proceeds by computation on attributes, where recognition of these attributes requires prior recognition of the category itself, is logically incoherent, as Rosch recognises. If you can't identify something as a wing independently of identifying it as part of a bird, you can't use identification of wings as a route to the identification of birds. Thus Rosch's structural principles play no part in category recognition.

The process of category formation in individuals would be not much less circular than the process of category recognition if proceeding along these lines. If the formation of categories is the result of computation of cue validities for attributes then again the attributes must be able to be individuated prior to, or at least independently of, the category they belong to, on pain of blatant circularity. But of course, as Rosch's third argument concedes, many if not all attributes are themselves categories. How are these categories formed? Presumably for the same reasons: computation over attributes. But now we are in an infinite regress, since these attributes are also categories and we have to ask in turn how these categories are formed, and so on.

The situation is not actually much improved if we accept Rosch's claim that she is dealing with category formation 'in the culture' rather than in the individual. For the coherence of her account still depends on the assumption that attributes can be individuated independently of their categories — attributes must be logically prior to categories — and this opens the way to the regress of the previous paragraph. In fact, this appeal to a culture is something of a red herring. A culture, in this context, is, I suppose, a large group of individuals speaking a common language and living in roughly similar environments — a speech community. Presumably Rosch's reason for invoking this notion is to capture the fact that individuals in such a community are heterogeneous in many respects, and so to focus on just one of them would mean ignoring other relevant factors scattered elsewhere within the community.

But exactly the effect that she needs can be gained by making a familiar idealisation: instead of the relevant factors being dispersed randomly throughout the community (perceptual properties, functional requirements, the whole range of human activities and intentions) imagine them all gathered in one individual, one of many such who make up a completely homogeneous speech community. This done, we now have something very like that familiar character, the ideal speaker-hearer, or more accurately, the ideal language-learner. He has available to him everything that in real life would be collectively available within the speech community and dispersed unequally among its individual members. As far as I can see, to talk of the formation of categories within a culture is equivalent to talking about the formation of categories by an ideal speaker-hearer of this sort. It is an idealisation of exactly the same order as the idealisation of the instantaneous acquisition of language by a learner (Chomsky 1976:15).

If this is so, then Rosch does not avoid the problems of her account by moving to the level of cultures as the domain of category formation, since for the equivalent case, the ideal speaker-hearer, we have exactly the same problem as before: how does the process of category formation get started?

The only way to break out of this regress, and restore some vestige of explanatory adequacy to the theory would be to claim that at some point in this reduction we arrive at categories or attributes which are ultimate in the sense that they are 'givens' for the category-former and not the result of any prior process of computation: other categories are built up in turn by computation over these givens in something like the way Rosch has described. In some areas this is quite plausible, in particular for the category 'physical object' and other relatively fundamental categories which, as we saw, it is plausible to maintain are derived via universal perceptual or cognitive attributes. But if we try to extend this to all categories, we are faced with the problem of accounting for functional and relational attributes which do not have the kind of cognitive or perceptual basis which would be needed to carry this pattern of explanation through.

Our earlier discussions indicate that as well as perceptual attributes, in the widest sense, at least three other kinds of attributes are important to the way we regard objects: relational attributes like 'large', 'small', 'slow', 'fast' and such like; behavioural attributes: the kind of behaviour that is characteristic of a thing – dogs bark, birds fly and so on; and functional attributes: how we interact with objects, what we use them for, what their personal or social significance is. We sit on chairs, eat from tables, drink from cups, ride in cars and so on. (To this might also be added attributes like location in a fuller analysis — it seems quite important to an understanding of the term that, for example, 'chairs' and 'tables' are characteristically found in dwelling places, and it seems particularly to be important to the category of 'furniture' in general.) In the case of perceptual attributes like 'red', 'straight-edged', 'rough-textured' and so on, it is plausible to maintain that there is a fairly direct relationship between our perceptual system and the attribute in question, and hence to maintain that they are givens out of which categories could be constructed. In the case of behavioural attributes there is also a substantial perceptual component, presumably, but there is no such direct relation. The same is true of some functional attributes as well: at some level the notion of 'sit-on-able-ness' must make reference to various motor gestures, the sense of one's weight being supported by something that resists gravitational pressure, or something like that; but these are themselves fairly complex attributes. We are apparently faced with a dilemma: to attempt to go ahead and just regard these behavioural or functional attributes as simple constructions from more basic perceptual attributes would seem to be an exercise of unjustifiable Humean optimism. But to regard them as basic in their own right in the same sense that perceptual attributes are basic seems either false, if construed as a claim that we have concepts like 'fly' or 'sit-on-able' as part of our original stock of (innate?) concepts, and empty or trivial if it is a claim that there must be *some* translation of these concepts into some more basic vocabulary of perceptual or cognitive concepts. Since this translation is largely inaccessible to us the claim is either empty, because it is untestable; or trivial, because it is merely equivalent to the claim that we can understand what is conveyed by these attributes, which is hardly a fact which is in dispute.

There is, fortunately, an alternative approach to this problem, along these lines: when attempting earlier to describe the principles by which particular lumps of the physical were to be regarded as nameable, we allowed ourselves considerable latitude with respect to the individuation of attributes, since we took the notion of functional or behavioural salience for granted. The reasoning implicit in this move was as follows, and it is also appropriate here: as human beings, our physical and social (in a narrow sense) structures mean that we interact with objects and people in regular ways. We eat, drink, walk, sleep, notice things moving, growing, making a noise and so on. To say that some object or attribute of an object is salient is simply to say that it plays a recurrent role in this daily transaction between us and the world. That is not to say that any such attribute is primitive in the sense that it could not be broken down into more basic elements, but just that for the purposes of our daily life we do not do so. We regard (if we do) 'sit-on-able-ness' as a simple attribute of this sort even though we could break it down into further components if we wanted to.

It seems likely, in fact, that even Quine, parsimonious though he is in what he gives away to the constructor of theories, would have to allow us to take these attributes for granted. For notions like agency, and the function or purpose of objects within the space of human (or other) activities are precisely the kind of common ground which a radical translator (or a child) can and must rely on. If he could not interpret the phenomena presented to him by an alien culture in this way in the first place, he would not have any grounds for thinking that he was dealing with communicating creatures at all. He would not know whether what he was trying to 'translate' was even a language if he could not construe the behaviour of its 'speakers' along these familiar dimensions, at least in some measure.

We can then, I suggest, legitimately take these attributes as basic, *pro tem*; and for the purposes of this rational reconstruction, as prior to the formation of categories, even though it is arguable that they are themselves the result of some process perhaps like the one discussed by Rosch. When viewed in this way, Rosch's findings that basic level categories have a higher cue validity than others should be seen as empirical confirmation of the feeling that some levels of categorisation are more informative than others with respect to our way of interacting with the world, and with respect to our perceptual apparatus. But her findings do not constitute a complete explanation of category formation as such, we must concede, for we have had to grant the prior existence of some categories, which have to be taken as givens.

However, for the case that we have described, where a given 'attribute space' can be assumed, Rosch's cue validity explanation for the formation of categories can be seen as complementary to the principles of individuation or nameability sketched earlier: these principles, if they are correct, pick out the range of possible individuals – the range of objects which could be named; and Rosch's principles show which individuals, in a particular situation, will be named: how actual individuals, grouped by similarity into categories, are chosen in response to psychological and cultural preferences. It is even possible that some aspects of the principles of individuation, though not all, are actually the equivalent, at the level of individuals, of a cue validity explanation.

(This is not surprising: as we remarked, it makes no sense to talk of picking something out and *then* assigning it to a category. Things are always picked out *as* such-and-such.) For example, it seems likely that the principle stating that a group of independent objects counted as a nameable only if they jointly fulfilled some function not fulfilled by any subgroup of these objects is equivalent to the claim that such a collection of objects would have a greater composite cue validity under these circumstances than the sum of the cue validities of its components. Similarly, any subpart of an object, if not salient in appearance, function or behaviour, could not have a cue validity that was equal to or greater than that of the cue validity of the whole: thus no more information would be carried by a category formed around this subpart than would already be carried by the category formed around the whole. But though this might seem to raise the possibility of eliminating one set of principles by deriving them from the other, this cannot be done completely: the principles of individuation state, for example, that any independent object could in principle be named: but clearly very few such objects or collections of objects actually are named. Likewise, things that are regarded as different in some respects can still be grouped into the same category. This is the point at which Rosch's principles begin.

V

Whether Rosch would be sympathetic to the construal of basic attributes given above, I do not know. Her discussion of the role of objects in events (1978:43-6) suggests that she might, but this position is at least prima facie in contradiction to the views stated in the quotation given earlier, where she appears to countenance the possibility that attributes can be recomputed or revised after the process of category formation is completed, so as to make the category system appear more 'logical and economical'. On our interpretation of her principles this is not a possibility.

Even if our reconstruction of the notion of basic attributes, or a given attribute space can be sustained, there must still be added a caveat to the interpretation of Rosch's results along these lines. It is still the case, even when re-interpreted as above, that some of the attributes offered by Rosch's subjects cannot play the part demanded of them in the process of category or prototype formation.

With some simplification, we can regard perceptual attributes as representable by 1-place predicates (we regard them, rightly or wrongly, as belonging to objects), functional attributes as 2- or more place predicates, where one of the places is occupied by us — a functional attribute is a relation between us and an object, like 'sit-on-able-ness'. But attributes like 'small' or 'large' are relational in a different way: they are 2-place relations holding between individual objects and either other objects, or some implied standard of comparison. Even granting some kind of primitive status to the first two kinds of basic attribute and their consequent role in cue validity computation, we could not grant relational attributes of this latter type a similar role in the formation of categories, for they are only interpretable once categories have been formed. Only if these attributes are interpreted as, for example, 'large by comparison with us' (as perhaps for 'horses' or 'mountains'), in other words, if they are interpreted along the same logical lines as functional attributes could they fulfil this role.

Since we do not know the relative proportions of these kinds of attribute in Rosch's obtained listings, it is not clear if, when the cue validity measures are corrected to take account only of those attributes which can plausibly be regarded as category independent, the results she obtained would still hold. If the general lines of the theory are correct, they should do, but this is not something we can be sure of without further information.

There is still a further problem with Rosch's explanation for the formation of categories, however. Our interest in the principles by which categories are formed resulted in part from the possibility that we could base an explanation for some of our judgements of entailment etc. on them. The general pattern of such an explanation was to be along the lines

(i) ⌜As are Bs⌝ is true because everything that is a member of the category named by A is also a member of the category named by B.

(ii) This in turn is because of . . .

where the theory describing the principles of the formation of categories was supposed to fill in these dots, and supply a reason why the relationship between categories should be this way. When Rosch's theory is seen in this role the explanation is completed in these terms: every member of A is a member of B because either:

(i)   most of the attributes of a B are possessed by every A (where A is a subordinate category and B is a basic category) – spaniels possess most of the attributes characteristic of dogs.

or:

(ii) every A shares at least one attribute with B or shares an attribute with some A' which shares an attribute with B (where A, A' are basic level categories and B is a superordinate).

Part (ii) is a reflection of the fact that there may be no features common to all the members of a superordinate category and hence no set of features characteristic of the superordinate, but that the prototypical members will share some features which are often taken (wrongly) to be characteristic of the category as a whole and non-prototypical members will overlap the prototypes at at least one point. Thus a hatstand may not share any of the central core of features associated with 'furniture' but it will share some features with chairs, tables and the other prototypical items of furniture from which these central features are abstracted.

Rosch's account derives category membership, then, from both common attributes (subordinate and basic level) and family resemblance (basic and superordinate level). Categories at all levels though, are supposed to be formed for the same reason: maximisation of cue validity. The difference in levels is a reflection of the structure of the real world. But for those categories at the superordinate level whose internal structure is as described by the family resemblance theory, there is some difficulty, to say the least, in seeing how this could take place. Consider: the original family resemblance account was supposed to show how something can be a member of a category even when there are no features defining of or criterial to the category. But if categories are supposed to emerge from the fact that some co-occurring bundles of attributes have a higher composite cue validity than others, and this in turn is due to contingencies occurring in the perceived or functional world, then family resemblance categories should never arise having the extension that they do, for the simple reason that the required co-occurring bundles of attributes simply do not exist: that they do not exist is the whole point of the family resemblance theory.

Remember that cue validity for categories is a measure of two factors:

the extent to which cues to category membership are available at all (attributes common to the category) and the extent to which those cues are not misleading (attributes which do not belong to other categories). (1976:34-5)

Rosch appears to be assuming that, although the basic level of categorisation is that at which there are most attributes in common, there will nevertheless be some attributes in common to the members of a superordinate. But her results show that in at least one case this is not so, and in all other cases there are only a very few common attributes (adapted from 1976:391):

Superordinate Category	No. of Attributes in Common (edited attributes)
Musical instrument	1
Fruit	3
Tool	3
Clothing	2
Furniture	0
Vehicle	1

For the cases like 'furniture' — for the true family resemblance cases, that is — Rosch's principles would not work: if anything, they would predict that such categories could not exist, or at best, would contain just the prototypes of the actual category — which generally do share some common features — for there are no cues valid for the whole category. The only cues that would have a significant cue validity would be those common to several prototypes — but they are not sufficient to generate a category containing all the peripheral members as well. It is clear then, that Rosch's principles of category formation are only completely tenable for basic and subordinate level categories, and only partially for the superordinate level.

Does this affect the character of the explanation for these judgements of entailment based on categorial frameworks that we were trying to put forward? At the level of subordinate and basic categories it does not, but at the superordinate level the explanation is not complete, for it gives us no reason why such categories should be formed at all, at least when they are like 'furniture'. It seems plausible that for other superordinate categories like 'animal', there are a sufficient number of shared attributes for Rosch's explanation to apply. Whereas membership between subordinate and basic categories was explained in terms of our

Theories of categorisation

beliefs about the sharing of perceptual and functional attributes, membership of some superordinate categories need not involve such shared attributes. We need some other explanation for how they are formed.

Note

1. It is possible that Quine has simply changed his mind, of course, as argued by Chomsky (1976:187). Gibson (1980) argues that this is not the case, but it is difficult to reconcile the positions taken in the two references cited, it seems to me.

5   VERBS, PROTOTYPES AND FAMILY RESEMBLANCES

I

It is natural to ask, meanwhile, in the light of the results obtained by Rosch and Berlin, whether verbs display any of the same properties as the type of noun we have looked at. Do they, that is, map wholly or partly onto a taxonomic structure? If so, do the relations between categories and their members show the prototype effect, and could similar reasoning be produced to show why this should be so? If this turns out to be the case it would be an interesting result, for there is no *a priori* reason to expect it to be so: after all, although the categories named by the nouns we have looked at are by and large observable concrete entities, the categories – of events or actions rather than objects – named by verbs are far more complex and abstract, depending on factors which are often institutional or cultural, or to do with hypotheses about personal motives and intentions. One man's taking the life of another, for example, can be classified as 'murder' if done intentionally, as 'execute' if carried out as an officially sanctioned act of revenge in the appropriate circumstances, or as 'manslaughter' if done accidentally. There is usually nothing intrinsic to or observable in the nature of the act itself to determine which of these it will be.

Let us begin with the strongest hypothesis: that all verbs are organised into a single taxonomic structure. If this is so, then on the highest level we would expect to find a 'unique beginner' – a verb of which (since our data are, at this point, judgements of entailment) all other verbs are hyponyms. However, it seems clear that there is no such verb in English (Lyons 1977:298), though 'do' and 'be' possibly come close. In the light of Berlin's observation that it seems often to be the case that the unique beginner category is unlabelled, this fact of itself might not be too disconcerting. But it does not seem that any obvious candidate for a covert category fulfilling this role is at hand: it is difficult to conceive of some category of which both 'do' and 'be' could be members. It seems safe to conclude that if we are dealing with taxonomic structures at all, we are dealing with several different ones, headed by 'do', 'be' and possibly others, and not with a single integrated structure.

(There is in fact an obvious commonsense explanation as to why if all nouns or all verbs were organised into a single taxonomy, the unique beginner category would be unlabelled. For to describe something by the label for that category would entail only that it was compatible with being describable by any other of the labels of the taxonomy; i.e. any of the members. This would be tantamount to saying simply that it was a thing or an action or an event: not a particularly informative statement in most situations. On the uncontroversial assumption that there is some trade off between lexical structure and informativeness, there would simply be little use for a label for an all-inclusive category.)

A more plausible parallel between verbs and nouns, pursuing our amended hypothesis, is that corresponding to 'life form' categories would be those labelled by relatively primitive verbs like 'cause', 'make', 'become', 'act' and perhaps others like 'move' or 'say'. All of these have large numbers of hyponyms with little else in common between them. If this is so, then we might expect to find that corresponding to the generic or basic object level were verbs like 'kill', 'look', 'walk' and so on. Such verbs have been singled out by Dixon (1971) for a comparable role as 'nuclear verbs'; Austin (1961) also mentions what seems like a similar notion. This all seems fairly plausible, and so too does a further parallel: corresponding to the 'specific' or subordinate level will be hyponyms of 'kill', like 'murder', 'assassinate', 'execute' and 'massacre'. Thus, temporarily assuming that 'do' is the unique beginner of the class including 'kill' we get a picture something like:

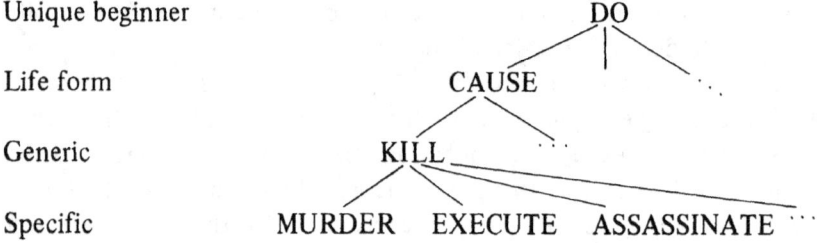

Unique beginner	DO
Life form	CAUSE
Generic	KILL
Specific	MURDER EXECUTE ASSASSINATE ···

We might even postulate a varietal level: e.g. 'execute' might have as hyponyms 'guillotine', 'garotte', 'hang', etc. At this level of detail the picture is not too unconvincing and seems comfortably parallel to the results for folk-biology and other domains. But when we attempt to explore further we very quickly run into difficulties. Varietal categories are not invariably included in a particular specific: to guillotine someone is not necessarily to execute him, but could rather count as murdering, as many a gothic story bears witness. Similarly for garotting. And what of 'murder'? Varieties of murder might include shooting, stabbing, poisoning or blowing up. But from 'X shot Y' we cannot even infer 'X killed Y' with any certainty and *a fortiori* not 'X murdered Y'. Using the means to murder does not guarantee achieving the ends.

Further difficulties beset our unique beginner and life form categories. We assumed that 'do' and 'be', for example, were unique beginners of presumably non-overlapping taxonomies. This assumption is highly questionable, however: in the first place, there is the fact that verbs like 'kill', which if we grant that they can be paraphrased roughly as 'cause to become dead', seem to make reference both to an action and a state. This being so, there is no clear motivation for incorporating them as hyponyms of 'do' rather than of 'be' (assuming that 'do' covers actions, and 'be' states) since either way it could be argued that an aspect of its meaning is being ignored by that classification. In the second place there are many verbs which can be used both transitively and intransitively with a consequent change of category: in the case of 'tire', for example, the intransitive use seems to make reference to states or change of states: 'John was tiring' (i.e. becoming tired) and therefore merit inclusion under 'be', whereas its transitive use refers to causation and therefore seems more accurately included under 'do': 'Running tired John'. If we widen our data base to include participles and deverbal adjectives then such changes of category become even more striking:

John closed the door (action, therefore 'do')
The door was closed (action and state, therefore 'do' or 'be')

It begins to look as if many candidates for unique beginner and life form categories are in fact categories against which their hyponyms are cross-classified, rather than being properly included within them as in a strict taxonomic structure. When we combine this observation with the earlier one on the mobility of our hypothesised varietal categories with respect to their superordinate specific categories it becomes clear that the hypothesis that verbs are organised in a manner parallel to nouns is largely false. (See also Lyons 1977:295-301.)

Nevertheless it seems that there are at least some groups of verbs which are organised in hyponymy sets reminiscent of the distinction between basic and subordinate level categories; 'murder', 'assassinate' and 'execute' all, in the relevant sense, entail 'kill' and so can be regarded as being subcategories of the category 'kill' — the category of events or actions of killing.

Just as in the case of nouns, where it seemed that to describe the relationships in question as 'proper inclusion' was correct but incomplete, it makes sense here to enquire further into the exact properties of this relationship: in terms of a spatial metaphor, are all instances 'equidistant' from the containing category, or do we have a situation analogous to that found by Rosch and her colleagues, where the category is internally structured around central instances, with less central instances grouped at increasing distances away? In other words, do verbs have prototypes?

II

In order to see whether the prototype effect obtained for verbs, I carried out a simple experiment which was in all relevant respects a replication of Rosch's original work (1973:131). The experiment, like Rosch's, asked subjects for subjective ratings of typicality; they were asked to decide which member of a given category was a more typical or more representative member of that category.

The preparation of the materials was carried out, from necessity, in a different fashion from Rosch's method. She used the Battig and Montague (1969) norms: a list of the frequencies with which members were given as responses to requests for members of categories. Rosch took six category members at roughly regular intervals of frequency. Since no similar source for verbs was available to me, eight hyponymy sets consisting of a hypothesised basic level and six hyponyms were arrived at *ad hoc*, with no guiding principle except that as wide a range of different types of verbs as possible should be covered. In fact it turned out to be quite difficult to find enough basic level verbs with a sufficient number of hyponyms. The final candidates were:

kill: assassinate, murder, massacre, commit suicide, execute, sacrifice.
speak: whisper, mumble, shout, drone, recite, stutter.
look: glance, stare, scan, peer, survey, squint.
walk: limp, pace, stride, ramble, march, saunter.
deceive: cheat, defraud, hoax, lie, decoy, mislead.
rub: polish, file, scour, grate, fray, scrub.
hold: squeeze, grasp, pinch, grip, hug, clutch.
burn: singe, toast, scorch, kindle, cauterise, brand.

These are probably not exhaustive lists of hyponyms, and they are not all uncontroversial: it might be argued for example that 'drone' is only metaphorically used regarding speech. While this may once have been true, I left it in on the grounds that it is commonly used as such (it figures in dictionary entries with this interpretation) and that in any case, subjects were told to ignore irrelevant sense of the words they were given, thus hopefully ruling out any problems caused by its application to aeroplane engines or mosquitoes. Other dubious cases were 'limp', which can presumably apply to running as well as walking, and 'lie', which some people feel can be used appropriately even when there is no intent to deceive.[1] The fact that the categories contained these doubtful instances does not really matter — Rosch's examples contained some equally dubious characters — and we would predict that if they really should not be there they would be rated as not very prototypical. Apart from these problems, in almost all cases the hyponyms are fairly accurately paraphrased by taking the containing category and adding some simple adverbial: for example, 'whisper' is 'speak quietly', 'mumble' is 'speak indistinctly' and so on.

The test was given in the form of a booklet in which subjects were asked to indicate their judgements of typicality by ticks on a 7-point scale. Thus the most typical item would be given a tick corresponding to 1, and the least typical, 7. Subjects were encouraged to use the whole scale as far as possible although there was no requirement for each item to get a different score from all the others. As in Rosch's experiment some examples were given to make the nature of the task clear: first the observation that 'apple' was usually judged a better 'fruit' than 'fig', and secondly, a sample group of verbs with an indication of my own judgements of typicality. These verbs were:

travel: walk, crawl, fly, drive, swim, cycle.

There was a slight difference from Rosch's method in that, although the order of categories and of items within each category was random, the order of presentation of the categories was not varied across groups, since only one group was involved. There appeared to be no correlation between the judgements obtained and the order of presentation. Other than this, the test was an exact duplicate even down to a paraphrase of the instructions to subjects.

The subjects were all undergraduates in their second or third week of an introductory linguistics course, and all were native British English speakers. Fifty-nine carried out the experiment and apparently had no difficulty in performing the task, although when invited for their comments afterwards a few people found that the precise ranking of *un*typical examples was rather arbitrary. Any responses which were incomplete or where the intention of the subject was at all unclear (two ratings for the same item, etc.) were discounted. These represented 2.33 per cent of the total. A chi-square test was used to measure goodness of fit between observed and expected distribution of responses. In all cases except one this was significant: 'kindle' marginally failed to reach significance (at five per cent level, df 6) by this test. Thus, for all of the words except 'kindle' there was a statistically significant tendency for the 59 judgements *not* to be distributed evenly or randomly over the 7-point scale.

The detailed results were quite surprising. In so far as I had any firm expectations at all, those expectations were that no very clear overall judgement of prototypicality would appear. The rather hazy grounds for this expectation were first that my own judgements were not straightforward (the 'travel' example was a rather judiciously selected one in this respect); secondly, that as the members had been chosen more or less at random — whereas Rosch's were chosen so as to get the widest spread along an independently measurable dimension (frequency of response) — I might quite easily have chosen those which were in fact all good examples, or all bad examples or all indifferent examples, rather than the mixture needed to demonstrate the effect (even if the effect were assumed to exist). Other grounds on which a negative result might be expected would be (i) if verbs are cross-classified against both overt and covert categories, as our earlier discussion indicated, there is no reason to expect the influences which form prototypes within taxonomic structures to be at work here, since we are not dealing with a taxonomic structure of any great depth. More simply, there does not seem to be any clear sense to be made of the notion of 'maximisation of information' here, assuming that Rosch is correct in claiming that prototypes are the result of 'cognitive economy'. (ii) Hyponyms are modifications of their category along a variety of disparate dimensions. In the examples chosen, the type of modification involved includes at least intensity (e.g. 'stare'), manner ('whisper'), instrument ('brand', 'grate'), reason ('execute'), purpose ('decoy'), volition ('mislead' vs. 'cheat') and causation ('kindle') as well as other more idiosyncratic properties. There is no *a priori* reason to expect any of these dimensions to be equated with more or less 'psychological distance' from the containing category than any of the others.

Nevertheless, when the mean rating for each item was computed, there was clear evidence that in each category, some members were consistently judged more typical of that category than others. The rankings, with mean ratings were as in Figure 5.1. These results compare very favourably with those obtained by Rosch, and for one item ('murder') there was virtual uniformity over what was the best example. The conclusion that the prototype effect obtains for verb as well as for noun categories therefore seems inescapable. People can reliably make judgements of the form '"murder" is a better example of "killing" than "execute" is'.

Figure 5.1

	1	2	3	4	5	6
look	survey 2.05	stare 2.80	glance 2.87	scan 3.25	peer 3.91	squint 6.05
kill	murder 1.10	assassinate 2.05	execute 2.82	massacre 3.28	sacrifice 5.22	commit suicide 5.33
speak	recite 2.57	mumble 3.46	shout 3.51	whisper 3.64	drone 3.98	stutter 5.35
walk	stride 1.86	pace 2.05	saunter 2.41	march 3.01	stumble 5.31	limp 5.37
deceive	lie 1.87	cheat 2.20	mislead 2.34	defraud 3.84	hoax 4.10	decoy 5.01
hold	grasp grip 2.03		clutch 2.45	hug 3.40	squeeze 4.36	pinch 5.30
burn	scorch 2.10	singe 2.61	kindle 3.90	toast 4.54	brand 4.80	cauterise 4.83
rub	polish 1.81	scour 3.80	scrape 4.21	file 4.70	grate 4.76	fray 5.69

III

The question that immediately arises is whether Rosch's explanation for the formation of noun prototypes can be extended to account for the data on verb prototypes. Recall that according to Rosch, prototypical members of categories are those which have the greatest 'family resemblance' measure: they share most of their features with other members of the category and fewest with members of other categories. Prototypes, like categories in general in Rosch's account, are formed so as to maximise their cue validities: the same principles underlying the formation of categories also underlie the formation of prototypes.

However, the character of Rosch's explanation for the formation of prototypes is somewhat different from that of her explanation for the formation of categories, in the sense that it is plausible to consider, as an idealisation, prototype formation as consequent to the formation of categories and attributes, thus avoiding the problematic regression encountered earlier. There is no logical problem in the idea of some mechanism, once given attributes and categories, computing family resemblance scores on the basis of these, with the resulting prototype effect. (There is, unfortunately, given Rosch's reluctance to involve prototypes directly in recognition or any other cognitive task, something of a problem in explaining just why prototypes should arise at all, given their apparent uselessness: principles of cognitive economy could reasonably be expected not to produce entirely gratuitous consequences.) So, if verb prototypes are formed in response to these same principles of cognitive economy, we should expect to find that our best examples were those which also had the greatest degree of family resemblance within that category.

In attempting to test this, however, we immediately run into some formidable difficulties. The basic one is that of isolating attributes which could form the features on which family resemblance is computed. For Rosch's subjects, the eliciting of attributes seemed a straightforward and reasonable task, resulting in lists like the following:

chair: legs, seat, back, arms
bird: feathers, wings, beak, legs, feet, eyes (Rosch *et al.* 1976:435)

which, though containing some problematic attributes, as we have seen, are clearly interpretable and not likely to provoke much disagreement. But it is not at all obvious that this would be so for verbs: categories like 'kill', as remarked above, are not readily describable in terms of perceptual or functional properties, but involve vastly more complex and more abstract attributes. The problem is even more acute for categories like 'deceive'. This emerged quite dramatically from a pilot study which was performed and was confirmed by the results of a further experiment.

These studies were both small-scale replicas of the Rosch and Mervis

(1975) family resemblance experiment. The procedure is as follows: subjects are asked to write down as many attributes as they can which are characteristic or typical of instances of particular objects, or in this case, events and actions. They have 90 seconds for each item. All the attributes which have been listed for it are combined for each item. Then each attribute receives a score, which represents the number of members of the category which are judged to possess that attribute. So an attribute characteristic of five members would receive 5, an attribute characteristic of only one member would get 1, and so on. The family resemblance score for a member of a category is the sum of the scores of each of its attributes. Obviously a member with many shared attributes will receive a higher score than one with few shared attributes, on the assumption that they all have about the same number of attributes. (Notice that this measure takes no account of dissimilarity of items to members of contrasting categories.)

For the pilot study, 13 subjects each performed the task on the members of the category 'hold'. They were also introductory linguistic students, native British English speakers, and had not taken part in the previous experiment. This category was chosen as being one of those for which there was no controversy over membership, unlike some of the others. Each subject had the items in a different random order, and each completed the task.

The results were extremely difficult to assess. The responses fell roughly into five categories: (i) synonyms or near synonyms (e.g. for 'hug': 'caress' and 'squash'); (ii) attempted definitions ('hug = hold affectionately'); (iii) the category name itself or some synonym of that ('hug' = 'hold'); (iv) connotations (for 'pinch': 'nasty, petty'); and, finally, (v) attributes of the type which would seem parallel to the sort of thing obtained by Rosch (for 'hug': 'using both arms', for 'pinch': 'with finger and thumb'). It is probably the latter category of attributes which ought to be taken most account of, though some of the others might reasonably be said to constitute a part of our understanding of the term. However, there are two further complications. In Rosch's experiments the attributes obtained from subjects were put through a certain amount of editing (p. 580). Attributes which were clearly false of a category were deleted and those which were clearly true of other members but for which they had not been listed were credited to those members. The total changes made in this way, says Rosch, were 'infrequent'. But if a similar editing is performed on the attributes elicited here, then in all cases over 50 per cent of the original attributes for each item have to be discounted, and in one case over 90 per cent. These were mostly attributes which could conceivably belong to a particular instance of the item but could not reasonably be conceived of as characteristic of it: e.g. 'hug' 'suggests aggression', as well as the large number of inappropriate responses in categories (i) and (iii). This ratio of changes could not be described as 'infrequent'.

The other factor is that many attributes were unique to a single member of the category. This means that if the family resemblance scores were computed in the same way as for Rosch's experiment, then a member could score highly simply by having been credited with more attributes than other members, even if none of those attributes was shared. Since there was considerable divergence between the number of unamended attributes each item received this could be a significant factor.

To try to overcome these problems several different methods were used to establish rankings and thus to see what correlations might hold. First, family resemblance scores were worked out on the total number of raw, unedited attributes. Secondly, they were worked out for those (unedited) attributes which were shared by two or more members of the category. Thirdly, they were computed on all edited attributes; and finally, on those edited attributes shared by more than one member, though in fact there was little difference between these last two scores. The rankings obtained were as shown in Figure 5.2, with the prototypicality rankings from the earlier experiment given for comparison.

Figure 5.2

Ranking by:	grasp	grip	clutch	hug	squeeze	pinch
1 Prototypicality	1	1	3	4	5	6
2 Family resemblance on all (unedited) attributes	4	2	1	6	5	3
3 Family resemblance on shared unedited attributes	3	2	1	6	4	4
4 On all edited attributes	3	2	3	6	1	5
5 On shared edited attributes	3	2	3	6	1	5

Spearman rank order correlations were performed for the comparison of prototypicality rankings with each of the other rankings. Since there were ties in the rankings the ties were broken both ways and all possible permutations were computed. The results were as shown in Figure 5.3. None of these results is significant at the five per cent level. Kendall's tau was also computed for these rankings, with the ties left unbroken. The results were as shown in Figure 5.4; none of these is significant at the five per cent level either.

Figure 5.3: Spearman Rank Order Correlations of the Rankings in Figure 5.2

1 with 2	a.	0.257
	b.	0.371
1 with 3	a.	0.542
	b.	0.657
	c.	0.600
	d.	0.657
1 with 4 (and 5)	a.	0.257
	b.	0.142
	c.	0.314
	d.	0.257

Figure 5.4: Kendall's Tau Coefficient of Rankings in Figure 5.2

1 with 2	= 0.207
1 with 3	= 0.357
1 with 4 and 5	= 0.214

These results were not very encouraging. The only correlations approaching significance were when family resemblance scores were given on the basis of the shared unedited attributes, thus including many things which strictly speaking are not attributes at all: items from the first four categories of response; synonyms, connotations and so on. Where Rosch's theory would predict a correlation – between the edited attributes scores and prototypicality – none was found to obtain at a significant level. However, this was only a pilot study, and only one category was involved. In the hope that perhaps better results might be obtained with more careful controls, and in particular if more explicit instructions were given about the type of attribute required, a further larger scale experiment was carried out.

For this experiment, the categories 'look' and 'kill' were used. Each item was printed at the top of a page and the pages were assembled into booklets containing six items, three from each category. The pages of each booklet were in a different random order. Twenty subjects carried out the experiment, each item being given attributes by ten subjects. The subjects were native British English speakers studying history and literature, who had not taken part in any previous experiments. The instructions were again a modification of those given by Rosch to her subjects: they were given an example of the attributes which might be listed for 'chair' ('has legs', 'you sit on it') and for a verb like 'swim' ('takes place in water') and whereas in Rosch's experiment they had previously been warned merely to try to avoid free association, here they were asked specifically to try to stick to properties which were characteristic of *all* instances of the item in question. Subjects reported that in fact this was quite difficult to do: the temptation for something like 'murder', for example, was to imagine a particular event, say a stabbing, and list the attributes of that. But of course stabbing is not a characteristic of all murders.

The resulting lists of attributes were not obviously better than those from the trial run. There was again a high proportion of synonyms, connotations and attempted definitions. Again during the editing process between 50 and 80 per cent of all attributes for each category was discarded as being either false of all instances, or a synonym, or true of the category as a whole (and therefore not contributing towards any difference in score between members). Again the rankings were based on three different scores: on total unedited attributes, on shared unedited attributes and on edited attributes (all of which belonged to more than one member). The rankings are in Figures 5.5 and 5.6; the measures of correlation for these rankings are as in Figure 5.7.

Again it is the correlation between prototypicality ranking and family resemblance computed on edited attributes which should prove significant. But although the results for 'kill' are suggestive, neither the Spearman nor the Kendall values are significant (five per cent level), and for 'look' the correlation is actually negative. This is in fact probably the most interesting and reliable result, for the close correlation between the rankings for all attributes and edited attributes, and the perfect correlation between shared and edited attributes, reflects the fact that the responses for this category were much better than for 'kill',

Figure 5.5

look	survey	stare	glance	scan	peer	squint
Ranked by:						
1 Prototypicality	1	2	3	4	5	6
2 Family resemblance on all unedited attributes	5	1	6	4	2	3
3 Family resemblance on shared unedited attributes	5	2	6	4	1	3
4 Family resemblance on edited attributes	5	2	6	4	1	3

Figure 5.6

kill	murder	assassinate	execute	massacre	sacrifice	commit suicide
Ranked by:						
1 Prototypicality	1	2	3	4	5	6
2 All attributes	1	4	6	2	5	3
3 Shared attributes	2	3	5	4	6	1
4 Edited attributes	2	1	5	4	6	3

in the sense that they corresponded much more closely to the kind of response obtained by Rosch – though still not very closely – needing less editing. Examples of the kind of attribute figuring here were:

> takes place for a relatively long time;
> takes place for a relatively short time;
> implies some difficulty;
> typically involves motion of head or face.

Nevertheless, even for this category it is impossible to escape the conclusion that family resemblance is not positively correlated with

Figure 5.7: Correlation for Rankings in Figures 5.5 and 5.6

look	Spearman	Kendall
1 with 2	−0.257	−0.2
1 with 3	−0.428	−0.33
1 with 4	−0.428	−0.33
kill		
1 with 2	0.257	0.20
1 with 3	0.085	0.20[a]
1 with 4	0.542	0.33

Note: a. The reason why the Spearman and Kendall coefficients are not matched seems to be that for a small number of individuals a large difference in ranks ('commit suicide') carries more weight for the Spearman test than for the Kendall test. It may be that Kendall's tau is the more suitable measure here (Hays 1963:652).

prototypicality, and hence is not a causal factor in the formation of prototypes.

This conclusion might still be resisted on several grounds. First, there is the fact that only six individuals in each category are involved in the rankings, as opposed to the 20 in the categories used by Rosch. It is arguable that for such a small number either or both of the statistical methods used would not produce reliable results: and there is certainly some truth in this. However, this situation is unavoidable given the fact that it is not possible to find more than a few extra members in each category which are sufficiently uncontroversial not to raise more problems than they solve − certainly not 20. In any case, as will become apparent later, other correlations can be found which are sufficiently consistent and impressive even with these small numbers to make the argument from the limitation of the statistical techniques not conclusive.

A second response might be that there is an important difference in scale between Rosch's original experiment and the one reported here. She used a massive 400 subjects, each subject rating six items, each from a different category, each item being rated by 20 subjects. I used 20 subjects, each rating six items, from two different categories, each item being rated by ten subjects. It is entirely possible that there was interference for subjects between items from the same category and that a larger scale experiment would yield better results. The difference in available resources make this a difficult proposition to test, however.

Even it it were possible for me to do so, I would still remain pessimistic about a larger sample producing any better results: both the experiment and the editing process were carried out carefully and the editing should have compensated to a large extent for any such interference. The fact that subjects evidently found it a very difficult task to perform at all would not be alleviated by having more subjects, and would not guarantee that more data would be more reliable data.

A third possibility might be to argue that all that is shown by this experiment is that asking subjects is a very bad way of getting at the characteristics or attributes of these verbs, which is difficult to deny. If we approached them in a linguistic rather than a psychological spirit, it might be argued, producing an analysis or a definition of each item and then computing family resemblance on this basis, perhaps we would find the correlation we are looking for. However, when this is attempted even on a small scale, it soon becomes obvious that for attributes obtained in this way the members of the categories in question have few if any features in common other than those which they all inherit from the containing category itself. This can be seen by inspecting some definitions of the members of the category 'look', for example:

glance	—	look at momentarily
stare	—	look at fixedly or intently
peer	—	look at closely, or with strain
scan	—	look at from one side to another
survey	—	look at all over
squint	—	look at obliquely with eyes narrowed

The adequacy or otherwise of the definitions is not at issue; these are all adapted from a standard school dictionary (*Chambers Etymological*). What is important is that they should all be at the same level of detail, so as not to bias the family resemblance score in favour of the one with the most separate attributes. On the assumption that something like such definitions is going to be our source of attributes, then whatever the finer details turn out to be, it is clear that the best example, 'survey', shares at this level only its category attributes with the other members. It follows that whatever accounts for this judgement of prototypicality has nothing to do with 'survey' having a higher family resemblance measure than other members, for it does not: they all have, if computed along the same lines, about the same measure. The other categories used in the prototype experiment do not seem to be any more promising in this respect, either, even where it is clear what is to count as an attribute.

It might finally perhaps be argued that family resemblance could be computed tacitly on the basis of attributes that are somehow different from those derived from paraphrases or definitions, or from subjects: attributes which are possibly not consciously individuated nor able to be articulated. While this is logically tenable, it seems to me that without some kind of evidence (which if the theory is correct, it will be difficult to obtain), this can only be regarded as an expression of faith in the principle of family resemblance, and carries a heavy burden of proof. The more natural conclusion to arrive at is that, whatever is the case for nouns, the prototype effect for verbs is not due to family resemblances.

IV

Rosch should not be represented as maintaining that family resemblance is the only factor involved in the formation of prototypes, though she clearly believes it is the major factor (Rosch and Mervis 1975:599). Among the other possibilities she mentions are

> the frequency of items and the salience of particular attributes or particular members of the categories (perceptual, social or memorial salience)

(though on the following page she rather puzzlingly claims that

> a measure of the frequency of items ... in the category is not correlated with prototypicality (p. 600)

referring to an unpublished manuscript: Mervis, Rosch and Catlin (1975)). It is of course quite possible, logically speaking, that noun and verb prototypes should arise via different processes. Nevertheless, it would be much more satisfying to have a single unifying explanation for them both. Could we, for instance, attribute prototypicality in both cases to the perceptual or social salience that Rosch talks of?

Unless salience can itself be quite directly explained, to say that prototypes are the especially salient members of a category is merely tautologous. Some independent account of salience is needed which does not indirectly refer to prototypicality. For some categories this salience is fairly convincingly describable in terms which make this pattern of explanation non-tautologous: it is reasonable to say that 'hawks' or 'eagles' are prototypical birds because they bear a heavy weight as a cultural symbol (especially for Rosch's American subjects, presumably). And it is plausible to maintain that 'murder' and 'assassination' are relatively high profile acts of killing, attracting more publicity and interest than suicides, say. But for other categories this kind of account is desperately implausible: what is so salient about 'tables', as items of 'furniture', or 'survey' as a type of 'look'? Here, salience seems merely a synonym of prototypicality and so cannot be an explanation of it.

For some examples on the other hand, there is the possibility that what may be involved in judgements of lack of typicality is the notion of an act being defective in some way or another; salience along a negative dimension of some kind. Thus 'squint' (though this is not explicit in the definition we gave) is a defective 'look', 'stutter' a defective 'speak' and 'stumble' and 'limp' defective 'walks'. They are all among those judged least typical of their category. Again, this theory is convincing for isolated examples but even for those categories from which it receives some support, it leaves us without an explanation for the best examples, which do not seem to be any less defective (if that makes sense at all) than their immediate neighbours.

Perhaps we can start a different tack. It is noticeable that the reaction of many people, when encountering the findings on prototypicality for nouns for the first time, is to say that they are due to familiarity. 'Apples' are a better example of 'fruit' than 'figs' because we are, on the whole, more familiar with apples than with figs. In a culture where the reverse was the case, the judgements might be reversed too. Although at first this idea seems obviously correct, like most such ideas it proves alarmingly difficult to pin down and make precise. Nevertheless, I think that this initial impression about the basis for prototypicality in nouns is essentially correct, and that from it arises the possibility of a unitary explanation for the prototype phenomenon in both nouns and verbs. So let us take a closer look at the objections to familiarity which are to be found both explicitly and implicitly in Rosch.

The first kind of objection would be that in the obvious intuitive sense of familiarity – the sense in which one thing is more familiar to us than another if we come into contact with it more often in our everyday lives – then the 'apple' and 'fig' example is not representative: some objects which are judged prototypical are much less familiar than unprototypical objects. Most of us are more familiar with chickens than with hawks, but we all regard hawks as more prototypical birds than chickens. This kind of objection can in fact be met in two ways: one to be described in more detail later, and the second, by pointing to cultural salience as a factor, in this particular instance at least.

A second kind of objection concerns the already mentioned difficulty of making clear exactly what is meant by 'familiarity': as noted, a reasonable candidate would be frequency of contact with objects or representations of objects, or perhaps frequency of occurrence of words. However, frequency of occurrence of words (it is worth noting that Rosch regards the members of superordinate categories as being words rather than collections of objects – Rosch and Mervis 1975:576), makes no sense in absolute terms (as Chomsky has often pointed out): and even with respect to particular contexts it would be a dubious measure of familiarity. One reason for this is the simple fact that a relevant context would usually involve presence of the object concerned; but that is just the situation in which the word would not have to be used, since pronouns would be the usual way of making nearly all but the first mention. Frequency of words as responses to questions about examples of categories ('what is an example of "fruit"?' – 'Apple') does correlate with prototypicality, as Rosch discovered: but it seems clear that this can be assumed to be a reflection of the prototype effect rather than the cause of it.

Frequency of items, on the other hand, while more promising, is more difficult to make experimental sense of, and in the few situations where it can be measured, it appears not to correlate with prototypicality. For example, in the work on the learning of artificial categories which Rosch mentions (Reed 1972), as well as in Posner and Keele (1968, reported in Reed 1978), subjects would rate objects as prototypical even when they had not appeared at all in the samples from which the categories were learned and therefore could not possibly be familiar. The categories in question were artificial ones made up of patterns of dots or letters, or schematic faces. It is of course rather risky to assume that what is true of artificial categories is also true of natural categories, but there is some evidence that similar facts obtain for at least some natural categories. For example, Anglin (1977:ch. 5) obtained ratings of both prototypicality and familiarity for members of four categories from adults – 'animal', 'bird', 'clothing' and 'food'. For each category it appeared that members could be divided into four groups: central (i.e. prototypical) and familiar ('cat', 'sparrow'), central and unfamiliar ('aardvark', 'vulture'), peripheral and familiar ('starfish', 'penguin'), and peripheral and unfamiliar ('centipede', 'kiwi'). Children between the ages of two and six, it was found, would recognise pictures of unfamiliar central animals, birds and so on, as instances of that category even though they were presumably unfamiliar with them, and even though familiar animals and birds like 'starfish' and 'chickens' would often not be recognised as members of their superordinate categories (though they were recognised as starfish and chickens). (Both Anglin and his subjects understand 'animal' as 'living being' rather than 'mammal'.)

Both the results from artificial categories and from categories like those used by Anglin are to be interpreted as showing that familiarity is not completely correlated with prototypicality: familiar things may be untypical members of a category, and unfamiliar things may be typical members. But it is wrong to conclude from this, as Rosch seems to have done, that familiarity plays no part of any importance in the formation of prototypes, for the kind of divergence between centrality and familiarity which was found is actually perfectly compatible with such an explanation.

Consider this picture of how the learning of categories might take place. Rosch's experiments (and Anglin's) show that the first categories to be formed, and the first to be named, are those which prove later to be basic level categories and prototypical members of superordinate categories. Peripheral basic categories and superordinate categories are learned and named later. Let us try to maintain the most obvious explanation for this. The most familiar objects are named first: 'cat', 'dog', 'chair', 'table', 'sparrow', 'canary', because they are the ones for which it is most useful to have a name, let us say. These are basic level categories. Later, superordinate categories are formed: they are formed around the basic level members already known, which become the prototypes of that superordinate. Other basic level items are added as members of a category: the question of whether they are in the category or not, and later, if they are in the category, whether they are central or not is decided in terms of how similar they are to the original prototypes, or to some abstraction from them.[2]

We have no information about when subordinate categories are learned other than that they are learned after basic categories, but if this account is correct, then the most familiar objects should again become the most prototypical for their subordinate category: if you have learned 'chair' from a particular type of armchair or kitchen chair then that type of chair when you learn its name would become the most prototypical armchair or kitchen chair for you. Clearly, as the child's horizons widen, there may be considerable readjustment here: he may quickly come to realise that his parents' Bauhaus furniture is relatively infrequently found within the community and therefore unfamiliar to many of his peers. Some information about what is regarded as prototypical may come from other sources. But at a certain level of detail such differences may never be noticed: my prototypical seagull may very well be different from your prototypical seagull, for example, if we have learned the term from different sources.

We can perhaps diagram this as follows. If the most familiar dogs, say, within a particular culture are collies then the formation of categories might proceed something like this:

```
Familiar instances    (1) Basic level              (2)a Superordinate
                               + 'cat', etc.→ ⎫
Rover, Fido, etc. ─────── 'dog' ──────────────→ ⎬      'animal'
                                                ⎭
                                               (2)b Subordinate
                                              ──→    'collie'
```

This will result in collies being judged prototypical 'dogs', and dogs being judged as prototypical 'animals'. Unfamiliar animals which are similar to dogs will be recognised as animals, while those which are not similar will not be recognised.

If the sequence of events is something like this fairly radical idealisation then there is no need for prototypicality to correlate exactly with familiarity at other than the highest level. Provided only that the most prototypical items are also the most familiar, then something might well be judged as closer to the prototype than another even when the latter is more familiar. For example, if your prototype of 'bird' is formed around sparrows and robins then you are likely to find hawks prototypical birds, since they bear a closer resemblance to them than chickens do, even if you are actually more familiar with chickens. Similarly, you are likely to judge an animal like an aardvark as a better example of an 'animal' than a starfish, on the grounds that it looks and behaves a lot more like familiar beasts like cats and dogs than starfish do. Always provided that the most prototypical members are familiar items, then this kind of non-correlation between prototypicality and familiarity is not inconsistent with the claim that the prototypes are formed around those members of the category which are most familiar within the culture. And when we look closely, it turns out that for all the items used by Rosch and Anglin, the items which were the most central were also the items which were the most familiar, either in the intuitive sense (since Rosch did not measure familiarity) or according to subjects' ratings in Anglin's work.[3]

The fact that prototypicality and familiarity are not exactly correlated all the way down the scale is therefore no barrier to the claim that the most prototypical items in a category are the most familiar. But there are some further consequences of this claim: in the preceding paragraphs we have talked rather loosely of forming categories around familiar examples. Thus your concept of 'dog' will be that which corresponds to the samples familiar to you (ignoring the kind of later adjustment and alteration that may occur on exposure to speakers from different backgrounds and so on), and, if the superordinate 'animal' is also formed around the same samples, as well as samples of cats and such like, then your concept of 'animal' will be closer to your concept of 'dog' than it is to 'armadillo', later on. In other words, the prototypes of a category will be closer to the 'meaning' of that category, in intuitive terms.

When we talk about two words like 'dog' and 'animal' as being close in meaning it is not clear whether we are talking about overlap of mental representations, overlap of extensions, or of beliefs about the objective similarity of the objects referred to. There are difficulties in interpreting 'closeness of meaning' or 'semantic similarity' in any of these ways. But whereas these difficulties are usually important, here we can, it seems, sidestep them: for there is ample evidence that people can make consistent judgements about 'similarity of meaning' in some broad sense, whatever it is in detail that is happening when they do it.

There are two kinds of evidence that prototypicality coincides with similarity in meaning to the category name. First, Rosch and Mervis (1975) discovered that prototypicality ratings predicted the extent to which a member could be substituted for the category name in a sentence: it is clear that 'sparrow' will substitute more readily than 'penguin' in 'A bird flew into the path of my car this morning'. It is also the case that if people are invited to make up a sentence about birds they are more likely to produce one like this than one like 'I saw the birds waddle across the ice floe'. This all suggests that 'sparrow' is more nearly synonymous with 'bird' than 'penguin' is.

Secondly, in an experiment suggested by those of Rips, Shoben and Smith (1973) Rosch asked subjects for their judgements of similarity, on a 9-point scale, between all possible pairings of a list of words including a superordinate like 'furniture' and all the members of the category. Thus subjects were being asked to judge the similarity between pairs like 'table' and 'chair' as well as between 'chair' and 'furniture'. 'Multi-dimensional scaling' computer programs exist (Shepherd 1962) which will display the resulting patterns of similarity visually, in various dimensions: thus two items which are judged similar will be represented as physically closer to each other than items judged dissimilar. Sometimes it is possible to infer from the patterns that emerge the semantic dimension on which these judgements are being made: for example, in the case of birds it is apparent that they are judged as being similar in respect of both size and domesticity (Rips, Shoben and Smith 1973:10).

Rosch obtained such similarity ratings for 'furniture', 'vehicle', 'weapon', 'fruit' and 'vegetable', from 15 subjects. She discovered that

> while the dimensionality of the scaling solutions was generally difficult to interpret, in all cases the category name and the most prototypical items appeared to be the most central in the scaling solution regardless of the number of dimensions or the rotation used. (1975: 503)

In other words, the prototypical members of the category were always closest in meaning to each other, and to the name of the category as a whole. Now, the fact that prototypical members of these categories are those with the highest family resemblance scores would predict the first of these findings, for degree of family resemblance is in effect one way of measuring degree of similarity. That is the correlation that Rosch was hoping to find. But there is, as far as I can see, nothing in the family resemblance account, *per se*, to predict the second finding, for it is perfectly consistent with *that* account that the category name — the superordinate — should be equally distant from all the members, or closest to the least prototypical member, or any of a range of alternatives. Unless some further assumptions are made about the meaning of the category name — for example that it consists of a disjunction of all the attributes of its members — which Rosch is careful not to do, or alternatively, if prototypicality is already taken as *a priori* synonymous with similarity, which it surely should not be (and which Rosch does not take it to be), then family resemblance between prototypes predicts similarity between prototypes but has nothing whatsoever to say about similarity between prototypes and the overall category name.[4] It is true that in some of Rosch's early work, and here, a spatial metaphor is often used in describing prototypes which might suggest this semantic similarity. But this is a misleading suggestion; if we are keeping, as we should, the notions of 'similarity of meaning' and 'typicality within a category' strictly separated, then there is not the logical connection here that there is between family resemblance and similarity.

On the other hand, if the learning of names for categories proceeds by way of familiar examples in the fashion described, then semantic similarity of category name to prototype would be an automatic consequence, since the category name is, as it were, attached to the prototypes rather than the peripheral members. The fact that this similarity exists can therefore be taken as support for the claim that prototypes are formed in this fashion.[5]

The exact relation between semantic similarity and family resemblance is rather complex. From the fact that prototypes are those members most similar in meaning to their category name it does not necessarily follow that they should also be similar to each other. (They could all be similar to the category name in different respects.) But it does follow from the fact that they are similar to each other that they should have a higher degree of family resemblance. In fact it is clear that similarity in the general sense must be taken as a notion logically prior to that of family resemblance: the latter can be constructed from the former but not vice versa, for in order to compute family resemblance you have to identify the same attribute as occurring in more than one member. But as our earlier discussion indicated, this is equivalent to saying that there is an antecedently given category consisting of manifestations of those attributes: in order to say that it is the *same* attribute in two different members it has to be assigned to the category. How is this done? — on the basis of similarity. Similarity is therefore prior to family resemblance.

The fact that family resemblance can be derived from similarity in this way, where there is the appropriate distribution of attributes, suggests the following hypothesis: the members of the category which are most prototypical are always those members which are closest in meaning to the category name itself. The category is in fact framed round the prototypical examples. We are now taking the step of explicitly linking typicality and semantic similarity. Family resemblance on this hypothesis is not always an automatic consequence of the process of prototype formation, nor an explanation for it, for it is entirely conceivable that some items might be similar to the category name each in different respects and thus not necessarily similar to each other, as pointed out above. In most of the noun domains we have looked at this is fairly unlikely, of course, but for the verbs I think that it is probably the usual state of affairs. (Notice that the properties which are common to all members of a category do not contribute to differences in family resemblance scores.) If there were no other properties shared by more than one member — as for some of the verbs — then similarity would obtain between the prototypical items — the most familiar — and the category name purely by virtue of the fact that the category name was attached to these prototypes: there would not have to be any difference in family resemblance scores — all the members would resemble each other to the same extent. But where items do share features over and above those present in all members of the category, then the prototypes will have the greatest measure of family resemblance and the items similar to the prototypes will have a greater measure of family resemblance than dissimilar items.

If it should turn out that judgements of typicality correlated with judgements of similarity for verbs as well, then it would be reasonable to propose the similarity of meaning hypothesis as the kind of unifying explanation for the prototypicality effect in both nouns and verbs that we were looking for. It would not, however, be terribly plausible in my opinion to propose that the mechanism by which similarity arises for nouns is also operating in the formation of verb prototypes: in particular, it is much more difficult to talk about familiarity for verbs — in what sense is 'survey' more familiar than 'squint'? And in any case we do not have the kind of data that we have for nouns concerning the sequence in which items are learned: it may be that the sequence is completely different or even completely unsystematic. It is more likely that, if the effect holds at all, it is simply the case that fewer additional features have to be added to 'kill' to get something synonymous with 'murder' than to get something synonymous with 'execute': a fairly direct interpretation of the notion 'similarity of meaning', in other words, unlike the case for nouns.

In order to test the 'similarity of meaning' hypothesis for verbs I carried out a third experiment. This was similar to those of Rosch and Rips *et al.* but simpler, for two reasons: first, that the computational facilities necessary for a full multi-dimensional scaling analysis were not available to me, and secondly, that in any case a full analysis of all possible pairs was not necessary in order to test the hypothesis. In fact the failure of the family resemblance scores to correlate with prototypicality would suggest that a pair of prototypical verbs would not necessarily be judged more similar to each other than a pair consisting of a prototypical and a peripheral verb. For these reasons, subjects were asked merely to rate the similarity between members and the category name, rather than also rating similarity between members and members. Thus they were asked to rate how similar 'murder' was to 'kill', how similar 'assassinate' was to 'kill' and so on, but not how similar 'murder' might be to 'assassinate'.

The same two categories were used as for the family resemblance experiment: 'look' and 'kill'. The subjects were given a form very similar to the one used for the prototype experiment and asked to rate the similarity of the members to the category name along a 7-point scale. All were British English speakers studying a variety of subjects. (With the accidental exception of two, there was no overlap of subjects between this and any other previous experiments, and in the case of the two who performed both this one and the prototype experiment over a year had elapsed between the first and the second experiment.) Both the orders of categories and four different random orders of items within categories were distributed approximately evenly among the subjects. Again they were encouraged to ignore irrelevant senses of the words, and to use the whole scale, but as before, there was no prohibition against giving two or more verbs the same score. Thirty-one subjects carried out the experiment.

A chi-square test was carried out for each individual item to test for goodness of fit between expected and observed frequencies. The pattern of responses for all items except 'peer' were significant at the five per cent level (df 6). The average scores were as in Figure 5.8. The rankings emerging from this and compared to the prototypicality rankings are as in Figure 5.9. Rank order correlations for 'look' are: Spearman 0.829, Kendall 0.733. The Spearman coefficient just fails to reach significance at the five per cent level (the significance level is extremely high for a small number of items such as this) but the Kendall score is significant. For 'kill', the correlation is of course perfect.

I don't think that there can be any reasonable doubt that these results demonstrate that similarity of meaning to the category name correlates far better with prototypicality than family resemblance does, and that they support the hypothesis that the basis for these prototypicality judgements is actually similarity of meaning with the category name. What people are doing, on this account, when making judgements about the typicality of a member of a verb category, is computing the amount of semantic modification needed to get from the category

Figure 5.8: Average Scores

look:	survey	glance	scan	stare	peer	squint
	2.58	2.80	3.10	3.23	4.10	5.68
kill:	murder	assassinate	execute	massacre	sacrifice	commit suicide
	1.45	2.48	2.90	3.74	5.55	5.84

Figure 5.9: Rankings

look:	survey	stare	glance	scan	peer	squint
prototypicality	1	2	3	4	5	6
similarity	1	4	2	3	5	6
kill:	murder	assassinate	execute	massacre	sacrifice	commit suicide
prototypicality	1	2	3	4	5	6
similarity	1	2	3	4	5	6

name to the member. If not much is needed the item is judged prototypical. The same, *mutatis mutandis*, must be true for nouns, though here it seems more likely that similarity may not be directly computed in this way, but can arise from the way in which noun categories are learned.

V

There are three facts to be explained concerning the phenomenon of prototypicality: (1) the emergence of some member or members of a category, or some abstraction from them, as the prototype(s) of the category; (2) the basis for judgements of relative typicality between members of a category; and (3) the subjective closeness in meaning between the prototypes and the name of the category. The view we have arrived at explains these as follows: for nouns, at least for those describing natural kinds and familiar concrete objects, prototypes are formed as a result of the learning process, particular members of the category being those most familiar within the culture and first associated with the category. This is not to claim that every individual learns every category in this way: prototypicality, once established, can be passed on to other members of the speech community. For example, when children are explicitly taught category names, or discover them from books or by other means, it is almost always via good examples of the category. Furthermore, personal experience can be altered or overwritten by wider contact later on.

Judgements of prototypicality for nouns are based on judgements of similarity to the prototype(s). In the case of categories the members of which possess readily discernible features this may take the form of family resemblances, but this is not necessary to this account and is merely one way of being similar. The fact that the category name is regarded as closest in meaning to the prototype follows from the way in which the category names are learned, being associated in the first place with the prototype of the category.

For verbs the situation is rather different. It is not clear how these categories are learned, though it is not impossible that the sequence of events should be as for nouns and thus the emergence of prototypes would have a similar explanation. However, at the moment it looks as if the prototypes of a category are simply those members which are closest to it in meaning, in the sense that it requires the smallest amount of semantic modification to the containing category name to produce an approximate paraphrase of them. Thus judgements of prototypicality within verb categories are judgements of similarity between the category name and a member, rather than between a prototype and another member. In the majority of cases, of course, these two possibilities will be indistinguishable, but nevertheless I want to claim that the reason why 'execute' is rated as more prototypical than 'sacrifice' is because it is closer in meaning to 'kill' than 'sacrifice' is, not because it is closer in meaning to 'murder'. If 'murder' is the prototype — the closest in meaning of all the members to 'kill' — then the second fact follows from the first one, but it is the first one and not the second which explains the prototypicality judgements. Given this account of prototypicality the closeness of meaning between prototype and category name follows trivially, of course.

There remains now the question of the exact relevance of the findings on prototype for the relation of membership and of inclusion by which the various categories are organised into a framework. Since the earliest work on prototypes it has been assumed that the effect demonstrated that categories 'do not have well-defined boundaries' (Rosch 1973:112) and that 'category membership is not simply a yes-or-no matter, but rather a matter of degree' (Lakoff 1972:184). Following Lakoff's lead, several writers have used Zadeh's (1965) fuzzy set theory to explicate the idea of 'degree of membership' in a set or category. Kay and McDaniel (1978) describe the semantics of colour terms by this method, deriving fuzzy set-like functions from the neurophysiology of colour vision. (However, their ingenious attempt to produce a formal account of the distinction between basic and non-basic colour terms has been found inadequate in various respects by Mervis and Roth (1980).) Coleman and Kay (1981) likewise equate prototypicality with degree of membership in a category and apparently endorse the applicability of fuzzy set theory to words other than colour terms (p. 27).

On the other hand, Osherson and Smith (1981) have attacked prototype theory precisely via its fuzzy set-theoretic formulation, arguing that under this formulation the notion of prototype does not allow the kind of compositionality which is required of any theory of word meaning. They take the notion of a prototype to entail the existence for each category of a function assigning to each member of the category a number between 0 and 1 indicating the degree of membership of that item in the category. The most prototypical members are those to which this function assigns a value close to 1. Then it is easy to show that combinations of the type 'pet fish' or 'red tree' do not have the prototypicality ratings predicted by their constituents under the appropriate fuzzy set theoretic operation. The operation in question they assume to be intersection, the degree of membership in which is defined as a simple function of the degrees of membership of each of the sets in question:

minimum (degree of membership in 'pet', degree of membership in 'fish') = degree of membership in 'pet fish'

That is, the degree of membership of an item in the intersection of two sets will be the lowest of the degrees it has in the sets individually. Although they did not test this experimentally, Osherson and Smith argue that this does not match our intuitions about such cases: for example, a guppy is not a very prototypical pet and not a very prototypical fish, but it is a pretty prototypical pet fish, contrary to what is predicted by the formula above.

It may be, in fact, that this particular objection can be met by associating this kind of semantic composition with some different set-theoretic function, as Kay and McDaniel do in their treatment of 'orange' as a more complex function of the intersection of 'red' and 'yellow' (1978:633). It is unlikely that Osherson and Smith's other objections could be disposed of in this way, however, and so it might appear that prototype theory faces considerable difficulties as a theory of word meaning.

This is not necessarily the case, fortunately. Osherson and Smith take their argument that fuzzy set theory is not consistent with certain types of compositionality as an argument against the validity of prototype theory *per se*, in any of several possible versions (pp. 54-5). But Osherson and Smith's observations, rather than casting any new doubts as to the status of prototype theories, instead, it seems to me, provide support for the alternative contention that it was misguided right from the start to associate prototypicality ratings with 'degree of membership' as reconstructed by fuzzy set theory. While it is certainly true that there are some terms for which it is possible to make judgements of the form 'X is Y to a greater extent than Z is', such as 'large', 'obliging' or even perhaps colour terms (hence the partial success of Kay and McDaniel's fuzzy treatment of them, which Osherson and Smith do not refer to), it seems obvious that this is not the case for the nouns and verbs that we have been discussing here. Categories like 'bird' are surely not graded in membership: penguins, chickens, ostriches and the like are *all* birds. The original significance of Rosch's findings was that although membership was not at issue, it was nevertheless not the whole story: as well as judging that a penguin and a robin are both birds, people can also judge that a robin is a better example, a more prototypical member of the category than a penguin. But the important point is that this is a judgement which can be made *over and above* the judgement of membership; it is merely clumsy to conflate the two, not a theoretical insight. Likewise, even though 'murder' might be a better, more typical 'kill' than 'commit suicide', it is not a matter of degree that both belong to the category 'kill'. Anyone who is in any doubt over that question simply does not understand what these words mean.

Thus membership and proper inclusion is indeed an all or nothing matter, at least for the categories we have been looking at. So Osherson and Smith's arguments do not count against the validity of prototype theory *per se*, though they do raise an interesting problem as to exactly what is going on in examples like their 'pet fish'. On the dubious assumption that a term like 'pet' is of the same semantic type as 'fish' and on the further (safer) assumption that the extension of 'pet fish' is represented by the intersection of the extensions of 'pet' and 'fish', then it will not be the case, on the version of prototypicality developed here, that judgements of typicality in the intersection have to be any function of judgements within the original categories. Judgements of prototypicality in 'pet' are via semantic similarity to prototypical pets, perhaps cats, dogs and budgerigars (pets are not a natural kind). Likewise for 'fish'. Judgements of typicality for 'pet fish' will naturally be in terms of similarity to prototypical pet fish. Since we assume that prototypes for combined categories such as these must be computed rather than pre-stored, for obvious reasons, we now have to ask how the prototypical 'pet fish' is decided on. And surely here again familiarity is the obvious answer: we consider which examples of the complex category are most frequent and most likely to be encountered. If guppies and goldfish are the most familiar pet fish then something will be judged as a prototypical pet fish to the extent that it is similar to these. But here too membership is absolute: if you keep a hammerhead shark in the bathtub as a pet then it is a 100 per cent pet fish, however untypical it may be.

Notes

1. See Coleman and Kay (1981), who demonstrate that the prototype effect holds for this subordinate category, too.

2. This might also provide an explanation for the phenomenon of overextension by young children, where a word like 'ball' is applied to an object like the moon. See Bowerman (1977) for some discussion.

3. The single exception to this was that 'hens' and 'ducks' were rated as being exactly as familiar as the most prototypical members like 'sparrow'. It is clear that these birds are regarded as relatively untypical because they are not salient fliers and they are domesticated: two features which jointly distinguish them from most other birds. This is where a family resemblance account may play a part in explaining prototype judgements, even though it is not involved in prototype formation. The features which are taken account of in computing family resemblance will be those which are derived from the most familiar members of the category, though, and so family resemblance and familiarity are connected. It could conceivably turn out in some cases of zoological categories that the features characteristic of the local common fauna were actually quite unrepresentative of the category as a whole, and that this would bias judgements of typicality so that they differed between people from different regions even where these people agreed on the overall extension of the category. Perhaps a New Zealander of the last century for whom the kiwi, the cassowary and the moa (all flightless) were common birds might well have rated chickens as on a par with hawks until he became aware of the fact that his environment was rather special.

Thus what really needs explaining in the 'hens' and 'ducks' case is not their lack of prototypicality, but their unexpected degree of familiarity. This is evidently due to the fact that they are domesticated fowl, for the most part, rather than wild.

4. The same point is implicitly acknowledged in Osherson and Smith's (1981) critique of prototype theory, to which we return below. They have to assume, for their discussion, that 'the point in the space for the term "bird" corresponds to the prototype' (p. 38): it does not follow from the (prototypical) prototype theory they describe.

5. It is somewhat ironic that Rosch should have apparently abandoned her (1973) view of the role of prototypes in learning — a view similar to the one taken here — in favour of a pure family resemblance account, which she stresses is not intended as an account of learning (1978:28).

6 SEMANTIC CATEGORIES

I

We return in this chapter to the question of semantic categories. As we said earlier, it is part of the business of a theory of word meaning to try to provide a list of the semantically significant groupings of words in a language, and also, if possible, to spell out what their characteristic properties are, and how they interact with each other, if they do.

In recent years, some proposals concerning the nature of word meaning have been made by Kripke (1972) and Putnam (1975b) which can be construed (though this was not their major concern) as an attempt to provide a theory of the semantic categories of 'proper name' and of 'natural kind word'. The main features of their arguments are by now quite familiar and will only be summarised briefly.[1] Kripke argues against the theory (which he attributes a version of to Searle (1969)) that proper names are understood by virtue of the fact that they are 'abbreviations' for some cluster of definite descriptions at least some of which are true of the bearer of the name. This cannot be correct, says Kripke, for several reasons: if we find out that this cluster of descriptions fits another person better than the one we thought the name referred to we do not then transfer the name to this second person, whereas it would seem we ought to on the cluster theory. Instead we adjust our beliefs about the original bearer of the name. The cluster of descriptions cannot provide a 'route' to the bearer of the name, as it is supposed to, for otherwise the name would refer to *whoever* satisfied the descriptions. Furthermore, more drastically, it could turn out that none of the descriptions associated with a name was actually true of its bearer. For example, Nixon might turn out not even to be a person, let alone an ex-president of the United States of America. Nevertheless, we would carry on using the name 'Nixon' in the same way: an impossibility if the cluster theory were true, as on that theory we would have to say that our understanding of the name had changed, whereas it seems more plausible that what has changed is simply our beliefs about its bearer.

The role played by descriptions, argues Kripke, is that one or more may be used originally to 'fix the reference' of a proper name. The reference of the proper name is then passed on through the speech community by a complex chain of intentions. But neither the original descriptions, nor any others are part of the meaning of the name in any sense, and they may turn out to be false without affecting the reference of the name.

Kripke suggests that the same is true of natural kind words like 'gold' and 'water'. Although we think of these substances as being associated with some cluster of properties (being yellow, heavy, etc.), it could turn out, claims Kripke, that none of these properties was actually true of the substance it is associated with. We have only encountered, let us suppose, highly untypical members of the kind, which have given us a false impression of its characteristic properties. Nevertheless, even under these unlikely circumstances, 'gold' and 'water' would still refer to the same substances as they do now.

Putnam (1975b) develops these suggestions, attacking traditional (and current) views about the meanings of natural kind words, and unlike Kripke, going on to propose a theory of his own about the native speaker's competence in this area.

First, Putnam attacks — as Quine did — the claim that the meaning of a word — its intension — is given by a conjunction of properties, jointly providing necessary and sufficient conditions for membership of the extension, and hence providing a definition of the term. This claim is fairly easily disposed of by arguments involving various fictional scenarios. Assume 'tiger' is 'defined' by the conjunction 'four-legged', 'black and yellow striped', 'carnivorous', etc. It is not too difficult to imagine a tiger satisfying none of these conjuncts, but we would still call it a tiger. Conversely, not everything which is four-legged, black and yellow striped and carnivorous is necessarily a tiger: it might be a freak lion, for example. And phrases like 'a three-legged tiger' or even 'a vegetarian tiger' are not contradictions, as a literal reading of the claims of this theory might entail. The relevant judgements are a matter of degree: it is more difficult to imagine a tiger which isn't feline than a tiger which isn't striped but, says Putnam, it is a difference of degree and not of principle (p. 267). We can even imagine, he says, a situation in which, with some resulting consternation within the zoological community, it is discovered that tigers were really sophisticated robots controlled from Mars. Or we could imagine, as Kripke suggested, that we have been mistaken about the internal structure of water or gold, so that it is actually not true that water is H_2O or that gold has atomic number 79. Of course, these situations are grossly implausible, but Putnam's point is that they are consistently describable in a way in which a situation in which circles are not round or in which an only child is a twin are not.

Putnam, therefore, is, as before, acknowledging that Quine is correct over many traditional examples of analyticity. Sentences like 'water is H_2O' or 'gold is a yellow metal' have all, at various times, been offered as prime examples of analytic sentences. But the fact that we can imagine these sentences being false without making too great an effort of imagination, shows that they cannot be analytic. However, Putnam is assuming that there are, or could be, some genuine examples of analyticity, for he needs the contrast between these examples, and examples which are genuinely unrevisable to make his point. As we established in Chapter 2, there are some analytic relations between words, even if they may not be of the necessary and sufficient type. I do not know whether Putnam would still endorse his original definition of analyticity (discussed in Chapter 1), which required both necessary and sufficient conditions, but in any case, for us to concur in the points he is making we actually need no stronger version of analyticity than the one we attempted to define at the end of Chapter 2. In fact, all that is really required is that there is some content to the intuition that some situations could not be consistently described without some consequent shift in the meaning or reference of the terms in question: it does not matter if the analytic relationship in question is actually used by speakers in determining extension or not.

However, the fact that we can conceive of tigers not being animals or of water not being H_2O does not mean that in some sense it is not a necessary truth that tigers are animals or that water is indeed H_2O. This apparent paradox can best be explained in the following way (this formulation is adopted from Schwartz 1980):

(1)   Tigers are animals
(2)   Circles are round

Both of these sentences are commonly regarded as necessarily true, or analytic. But Putnam and Kripke are arguing, in effect, that they are necessary in different ways. Let us assume that it is a matter of stipulation that circles are round, and that therefore (2) is uncontroversially analytic. This is supported by the fact that it is impossible, so it seems, to tell any kind of story, however implausible, in which 'circle' and 'round' have the same meaning they do at present but in which (2) is false. On the other hand, it is possible to do this for (1), as we have seen: it is possible to consistently envisage tigers turning out not to be animals. The fact that this is so demonstrates that (1) therefore cannot be analytic, unlike (2). Nevertheless, we still have a feeling that there is something fairly necessary about (1). For given that tigers actually are animals it seems impossible that we should find an instance of something that is a tiger but not an animal. If we examine, let us say, 1,000 putative tigers and we find that 999 are animals whereas the 1,000th is a drastically mutated insect then we would decide that although it looked like a tiger, the 1,000th 'tiger' was not the genuine article, but an interesting impostor. If we found a sufficiently large number of these impostors we might decide that 'tiger' did not name a unitary natural kind, that there were two types of tiger, but a single or a small number of counter-examples would not count as tigers at all.

Thus the apparent paradox is resolved when we see that a question like 'Could tigers not be animals?' can be answered in two different ways. If what is being asked is whether it could have turned out that tigers weren't animals, then the answer is yes. It is epistemically possible that this should be the case. But if what is meant is whether, given that tigers have actually turned out to be animals, we could find a tiger that is not an animal, the answer is no. It is not conceptually or, as Putnam and Kripke say, 'metaphysically' possible.

The notion of 'metaphysical necessity' is a 'new' kind of necessity. It is not identical with analyticity, as we have seen. It is not the same as *a priori* for things like 'water is H_2O' are the result of discovery. It is a synthetic, *a posteriori* necessary truth. The notion has some controversial consequences. For example, to say that it is metaphysically necessary that water is H_2O or that tigers are animals is to ascribe to water and tigers certain essential properties, properties which are constitutive of the natural kind in question. This is exactly what Putnam and Kripke maintain: all members of a natural kind share certain properties in common — a particular 'inner constitution' or 'origin' for example (although it may not actually be known what this is). If a particular example does not have these properties it is not a member of the kind. The same thing is true of individuals: given that Nixon is actually a person and has not turned out to be a robot, it is an essential property of him that he be a person, having particular parents, etc. As before, he could have turned out not to be, but given that he has not, if we imagine a robot Nixon we are not imagining Nixon *himself* as a robot, but something which is a robot and which looks and behaves like Nixon.

The traditional view of word meaning, then, on which understanding a word involves grasping an intension or sense which in turn determines the extension or reference of the term, is not tenable, according to

Kripke and Putnam. How exactly then, since we certainly think we know the meaning of at least some words, do we set about determining the extension of these words, if it is not via their meaning? Putnam's answer is simply that knowing the meaning of the word does not provide a recognition procedure for its extension:

> Everyone to whom gold is important for any reason has to acquire the word *gold*; but he does not have to acquire the method of recognising if something is or is not gold. He can rely on a special subclass of speakers. The features that are generally thought to be present in connection with a general name – necessary and sufficient conditions for membership in the extension, ways of recognising if something is in the extension ('criteria') etc. are all present in the linguistic community considered as a collective body, but that collective body divides the labor of knowing and employing these various parts of the meaning of *gold*. (p. 228)

This is Putnam's 'division of linguistic labor' principle, which he hypothesises to be true of all linguistic communities. If it is correct, the principle implies that knowing the meaning of a word does not involve being in the psychological state of grasping its intension, and that words as far as individual speakers are concerned do not have conjunctive definitions or any kind of 'intension', as traditionally conceived, circumscribing their extension. The extension of a term is determined partly by factors which may be unknown, but presumed to exist, such as inner constitution, and partly by the social processes described above. Putnam's explanation for how speakers can use a word successfully without having a perfect knowledge of its extension is in terms of 'stereotypes'. His criterion for a speaker's successful use of a word like 'tiger' is (a) that 'his use passes muster (i.e. people don't say of him such things as "he doesn't know what a tiger is" ...)' (p. 247); and (b) the (socially determined) extension of 'tiger' in his idiolect actually is the set of tigers. Notice that this criterion suggests that a speaker's use could pass muster, but still not actually be correct. The speaker may never know if he is using the word wrongly: the second clause is the 'realistic' element in Putnam's theory, and is relatively independent of the individual, determined by experts.

The minimum knowledge required in order to fulfil clause (a) is knowledge of 'stereotypical' tigers. In general a stereotype is:

a conventional (frequently malicious) idea (which may be wildly inaccurate) of what an X looks like or acts like or is . . . I am concerned with conventional ideas, which may be inaccurate. I am suggesting that just such a conventional idea is associated with 'tiger', with 'gold', etc., and, moreover, that this is the sole element of truth in the 'concept' theory. (pp. 249-50)

How detailed does a stereotype have to be?

> The nature of the required minimum level of competence depends heavily upon both the culture and the topic, however. In our culture, speakers are required to know what tigers look like (if they acquire the word 'tiger', and this is virtually obligatory); they are not required to know the fine details (such as leaf shapes) of what an elm tree looks like. (p. 249)

In general, as a native speaker, you know how much information belongs in a stereotype: exactly as much as would be needed to tell someone (who did not know already) what a tiger was:

> if anyone were to ask me for the meaning of 'tiger' I know perfectly well what I would tell him. I would tell him that tigers were feline, something about their size, that they are yellow with black stripes, that they (sometimes) live in the jungle, and are fierce. (p. 252)

Putnam offers a 'normal form' for the representation of word meaning, saying:

> If we know what a 'normal form description' of the meaning of a word should be, then, as far as I am concerned, we know what meaning is in any scientifically interesting sense. (p. 269)

The normal form description for 'water' is:

(3)
Syntactic Markers	Semantic Markers	Stereotype	Extension
mass noun	natural kind	colourless	H_2O
concrete	liquid	transparent	(give or
		tasteless	take
		thirst-quenching, etc.	impurities)

Everything except the extension represents 'a hypothesis about the individual speaker's competence' (p. 269). Semantic markers are suggested by, but not identical to, the theoretical entities postulated by Katz. They are 'category indicators of high centrality' forming 'part of a widely used and important system of classification' (p. 267). There is, says Putnam, a great deal of scientific work to be done in 'finding out what sorts of items can appear in stereotypes' and 'working out a convenient system for representing stereotypes' (pp. 266-7).

II

Kripke and Putnam's proposals have generated an enormous amount of discussion in the philosophical literature, though very little in linguistics. The existence of essential properties, or of actual natural kinds, the implications of the supposed necessity of theoretical identifications like 'water is H_2O' for the mind-brain identity theory and for the reference of terms within and across scientific theories are the subject of continuing debate. Fortunately, we need not involve ourselves too closely with these complex philosophical issues: for our purposes it is sufficient to assume that there is some content to our intuition that there are natural kinds, and to our feeling that there is a distinction between superficial and essential properties of objects, whether or not these intuitions accord with scientific fact. If these intuitions prove to be scientifically ill-founded, or inconsistent, that does not necessarily matter: for example, any explanation of the way we use colour words will presumably make reference to our intuition that colour is an inherent property of objects. The physics and physiology of perception tells us that strictly speaking this is not true, but that does not threaten the linguistic explanation.

However, even when construed as a linguistic hypothesis Kripke and Putnam's theories have been challenged. Chomsky (1976:46-51) rejects Kripke's claim that there is a category of 'metaphysically necessary' truth separate from analyticity. Chomsky argues that Kripke's examples of necessary truths are cases of modality

> de dicto rather than de re, rather like the statement that the man who lives upstairs lives upstairs (p. 47)

In other words, the necessities that Kripke describes are a disguised form of analyticity or tautology, involving linguistic connections between categories such as 'animate' or 'person'. He invites us to consider the sentences (adapted from Kripke p. 256):

(4) a Nixon won the 1968 election
    b Nixon is an animate object

Our intuitions are that a is contingently true and b necessarily true. But these intuitions are explicable, says Chomsky, because proper names are implicitly categorised according to the type of entity they refer to. 'Nixon' is implicitly assigned to the covert category of 'commonsense understanding' we call 'person'. (4) b is 'approximately' synonymous with:

(5) The person Nixon is an animate object

and the necessary truth of this, says Chomsky

> is a consequence of the necessary truth of the statement that people are animate. This necessary truth may be grounded in a necessary connection between categories of commonsense understanding, or an analytic connection between the linguistic terms 'person' and 'animate'. Under any of these assumptions, we need not suppose that an essential property is assigned to an individual Nixon, apart from the way he is named or the category of commonsense understanding to which he is assigned. (p. 47)

In other words, 'metaphysical necessity' — if it makes sense at all — is not involved in explaining our linguistic intuitions here.

This is an extremely difficult set of questions but it appears to me that of the two alternative explanations that Chomsky offers for the necessity of (4) b, one — that it is a disguised form of analyticity — is incorrect, while the other — that it is due to a 'necessary connection between categories of commonsense understanding' — can only be construed as a version of the position he is attacking. In order to try to establish this let us digress for a moment over the meaning of 'metaphysical' for Kripke.

Kripke says:

> Any necessary truth, whether a priori or a posteriori, could not have turned out otherwise. In the case of some necessary a posteriori truths, however, we can say that under appropriate qualitatively

identical evidential situations, an appropriate corresponding qualitative statement might have been false. The loose and inaccurate statement that gold might have turned out to be a compound should be replaced (roughly) by the statement that it is logically possible that there should have been a compound with all the properties originally known to hold of gold. (p. 333)

Nevertheless:

Given that gold *is* this element, any other substance, even though it looks like gold and is found in the very places where we do in fact find gold, would not be gold . . .

statements representing scientific discoveries about what this stuff *is* are not contingent truths but necessary truths in the strictest possible sense . . . present scientific theory is such that it is part of the nature of gold as we have it to be an element with atomic number 79.

In other words, what we know about the category of natural kinds is that a statement about their constitution — or some aspects of it at least — is, if true at all, necessarily true. This whole conditional is known *a priori*. But since we can only discover whether, for a particular case, the antecedent to this conditional is true empirically, then the antecedent is known *a posteriori*. The inference to the consequent can lead only to another *a posteriori* truth, therefore, since one of the premises was itself *a posteriori*. The reason why Kripke regards this type of necessity as metaphysical, I think, is that although our knowledge of these particular necessities can only be *a posteriori*, and thus connected with our epistemic systems, our knowledge that such a necessary relation holds between natural kinds and their constitutions or individuals and their origins is *a priori*: it is part of our understanding of what it is to be a natural kind or an individual, not a discovery about them. Particular properties, though, are discoveries. It is thus metaphysical, not in the sense of describing some ultimate but perhaps unknowable reality, but in the sense that it is something that we inescapably bring to the understanding of that reality; or to put it another way, it is part of our implicit definition of the concept of an individual that its origin is essential to it and of our definition of a natural kind that its inner constitution is essential to it. But our knowledge of what these origins or constitutions are for particular individuals is subject to all the vagaries of any other kind of empirical knowledge.

So metaphysical necessity is in one sense a kind of linguistic necessity, since it results from the connection between the semantic category 'proper name' or 'natural kind term' (provisionally treating this as a unitary semantic category) and the ontological framework of individuals and substances to which these categories are connected. Mackie (1976: 96), though he would not put the matter in these terms, seems to me to reach the same kind of conclusion when he writes:

> What we can call in Kripke's theory the necessities of constitution are not epistemic, not a matter of a priori knowledge, and not analytic; they do not arise from our having included 'having atomic number 79' in the meaning of the term 'gold'; yet they are in a remoter way based on the use of language. They arise from and reflect our intention of using a substance name, say 'gold', to refer to the stuff with the internal constitution, whatever it may be, of which we recognise (using our various ordinary criteria) as pieces of gold are samples.

In Chomsky's view, a name like 'Nixon' is already tacitly categorised as a personal name, making 'Nixon is an animate object' have 'approximately' the same meaning as 'the person Nixon is an animate object'. What sort of connection is this? It is not analytic in any straightforward simple sense, for the name 'Nixon' could obviously be used of statues or any inanimate object, and the two sentences above would not even 'approximately' be synonymous. Chomsky clearly means that 'Nixon' is categorised as a personal name in a particular application. Is this categorisation analytic when understood in this way? It does not seem to me that it is: although 'analytic' is not synonymous with *'a priori'*, surely anything analytic is known *a priori*. But if this categorisation is analytic, then it ought to be an *a priori* truth that Nixon is an animate being, or that Nixon is a person. You would know they were true simply by understanding the name 'Nixon' in this particular application. But arguments similar to those used earlier suggest that this is not so, for we are able consistently to envisage the possibility that Nixon should turn out not to be an animate being or not to be a person. And if Chomsky is correct this should be just as difficult as imagining that the man who lives upstairs doesn't live upstairs.

Chomsky's view also seems to imply that a name could not be used independently of an assignment to a category like 'person'. It is probably true that a name cannot be used without being tacitly assigned to some kind of category, even if an all-inclusive one like 'entity'. But it still seems possible to wonder quite sensibly what *sort* of thing the individual is who is the bearer of a name. (Self-evidently, this would not be possible if the fact that the name denoted the bearer was not known.) It is perhaps arguable that this is a parasitic use of a name, but even granting that not every name could be used like this, the fact that it is possible at all is problematic if the connection between a name and a commonsense category is an analytic or *a priori* connection.

Finally, if Chomsky is correct in regarding 'Nixon is an animate being' as a disguised form of analyticity, then we are left with no way of accounting for the intuitive difference[2] between statements like 'circles are round' and 'tigers are animals' which we discussed earlier.

Chomsky's objections to Kripke's theory seem to spring from his belief that it entails that things have essential properties independently of *any* framework of description or categorisation (p. 46). If this is the correct interpretation of Kripke's notion of 'metaphysical', then I share Chomsky's difficulties with it. But the quotations from Kripke (and from Mackie) given earlier suggest that this is not an accurate reading of him. Rather, things have essential properties with respect to our conceptual framework, not in the shallow sense that properties are essential to them only relative to a particular description, but more deeply, via the recognition of them as *things* or as members of kinds in the first place. And if this is so, there does not seem to be any reason why Chomsky's other alternative of a 'necessary connection between categories of commonsense understanding' should not be regarded as equivalent to Kripke's metaphysical necessity. The reason why 'Nixon is an animate being' seems to express a necessary truth is that Nixon is a member of a natural kind for whom animacy is an essential property.

Putnam (and Kripke) have also been attacked by Katz (1975) who mounts a valiant defence of his theory against Putnam's criticisms. On Katz's theory:

(6) Cats are animals

is straightforwardly analytic. If it turns out that cats are in fact robots, as in Putnam's science fiction story, this does not show that (6) is false, according to Katz — it cannot be, for it is analytic. Rather:

> If Putnam's story about the things we have been calling cats turning out to be robots were true, it would follow simply that there never were any cats. (p. 76)

But if that is the case, how could we have referred to these automatons successfully by the term 'cat'? Katz's answer to this is that we have been using the term 'cat' 'referentially', in the sense of Donnellan (1966); that is, a use in which a term (a definite description, in the original version) can be used to refer by a speaker even though it is not actually true of what is referred to (Katz 1975:97).

This seems to be somewhat implausible. If Katz is willing to grant that cats might turn out to be robots, then he is also presumably willing to grant that water might turn out not to be H_2O and that gold might turn out not to have atomic number 79. In fact, any natural kind might turn out to have different properties. Let us suppose that at least one of the conjuncts in the analytic definition of all such terms (on Katz's theory) turns out to be false. Then the entire conjunction is false and so 'there never were' any genuine examples of any of these kinds. We have all been using these terms referentially all these years. The possibility of this seems a high price to pay to preserve the analyticity of (6). Furthermore, consider the occasion during this benighted period when I use the term 'cat' mistakenly to direct your attention to a dog. On Katz's theory there is now no way to distinguish this case from the normal case on which I was using 'cat' to refer to cunning feline automata: since there are no cats, both uses must be referential.

On Katz's theory, when cats turn out to be robots, we must either stipulate a change of meaning of 'cat', or coin a new term (p. 98). On Putnam's theory we carry on using 'cat' but have revised our beliefs. It seems to me that our intuitions side firmly with Putnam here. When it was discovered that whales were mammals and not fish they were still called whales. And there was surely no stipulation of a change of meaning: it seems in fact perfectly possible for someone to have used the term 'whale' properly – to understand its meaning (via a stereotype) in any straightforward way – without knowing either that it was a mammal or that it was not a fish (perhaps believing that it was some separate type of creature). The picture in which we simply change our beliefs about whales seems much more plausible than Katz's alternative.

Katz's discussion of 'blue lemons' also leads to difficulties for his position. Putnam had argued that 'lemons are yellow' cannot be analytic because of the possibility that we might discover that normal lemons were in fact blue, but that they all suffered from a particular disease making them appear yellow. Katz concedes that 'lemons' must refer to 'normal lemons' and says that

(7)   Normal lemons are yellow (when fully ripe)

is analytic

> Suppose ... we discover that these fruits are normally blue. The evidence on the basis of which we come to make this discovery is evidence about the essential nature of this fruit; hence, on Putnam's account, it relates to the scientific facts about the physico-chemical structure of lemons (and perhaps also about the character of the lemon disease). Since, therefore, this evidence does not concern the semantic properties and relations of words, it cannot influence the choice between candidate dictionary entries for 'lemon'. This evidence, new and startling as it is, can have no bearing on the correctness of the definition of 'lemon' already established on linguistic grounds. (p. 100)

The fate of 'lemon' is then similar to that of 'cat'. But what Katz does not notice is that on his account, the discoveries he discusses could not happen. Since (7) is analytic, it cannot be *lemons* which are discovered to be normally blue. That would be as impossible as discovering that the man who lives upstairs doesn't live upstairs or that circles are not round. 'Lemons are blue' will express a contradiction and a contradiction cannot be discovered by scientific enquiry. Again, it seems that our intuitions accord with Putnam's account better than with Katz's, for both in science and in everyday life we make discoveries which lead us to believe that we were wrong about the properties of some kind or some object. But we are still working on the *same* kind of object; we do not discover that there never were any of the former type and that we are dealing with a completely new customer.

III

We have agreed with Putnam and Kripke that there is a semantic category of natural kind words having various characteristic properties; in particular, some of the properties that a member of a natural kind has will be regarded as essential to it. If we assume that among these properties may be included membership of higher level or more inclusive kinds: felines, mammals, liquids, etc., then some of the semantic judgements based on categorial frameworks of the type described in Chapter 3 will have an element of 'necessity' about them which others may not have. If the members of a categorial framework are natural kinds then membership and inclusion relations will be a matter of 'metaphysical' necessity: that is to say, the semantic category they belong to contributes an important extra element.

Of course, it may be that some words which do not designate a natural kind nevertheless behave linguistically like natural kind words. The relationship between, say, 'hammer' and 'tool' or between 'car' and 'vehicle' may be like that between 'cat' and 'animal'. On the other hand, it may be an analytic relationship: it may be part of the meaning of 'hammer' that it is a tool. Either way it is clear that the relationships implied by their position in their respective categorial frameworks is not the whole truth: the contribution made by their semantic category, whether this is 'metaphysical necessity' or analyticity, is also essential to a full understanding of them.

It is interesting that the frameworks involved seem to have the same formal structure, as regards number and nature of levels, even if they do involve words from different semantic categories. This also suggests that there are two independent factors at work here: the principles of categorisation discussed earlier, which are concerned, roughly speaking, with 'amount of information', producing taxonomies which reflect in the level of detail of the groupings they contain, our everyday human interests and preoccupations. These principles operate independently of the semantic type of the terms which name the categories, though the semantic type to which they belong also influences our linguistic judgements.

Before returning to the search for other semantic categories besides 'natural kind word', there are some points to deal with concerning the details of Putnam's proposals, even though we can agree with them in substance. An obvious question to ask concerning 'stereotype' is to what extent this notion overlaps with the notion of 'prototype'. In Rosch's later work (e.g. 1978) she seems to distance herself from the conception of a prototype as 'a specific category member or mental structure' towards an operational definition, based on judgements and reaction times, so that categories do not have prototypes so much as a relation 'more prototypical than' defined over their members. Under this construal there is no direct overlap at all, for Putnam's notion of stereotype is clearly meant as a description of a 'mental structure'. On the construal of prototypes as representations of particular members, or as an abstraction from some core of particular members which are adopted (closer to Rosch's original proposal), then the notion of prototype seems to be merely a special case of the notion of stereotype. It is a special case rather than being identical because there has only been offered evidence for prototypes in certain categories of word: some natural kind words and some words for artefacts and institutional concepts ('crime'). The evidence for the prototypicality effect in verbs, we found, could be explained on the basis of semantic similarity without postulating that particular members of a category had any special significance other than their high degree of similarity to the category name. Putnam, however, assumes that a wide range of words which do not fall into any of these categories also have stereotypes: 'witch' for example: virtually all words, he suggests, can have stereotypes.

Furthermore, the information constituting a prototype on our construal normally consists mostly of perceptual or functional properties, perhaps with some information about typical location for some categories. Stereotypes, however, can apparently contain various sorts of information over and above this type: from purely idiosyncratic or conventional facts to highly theory-laden items. This information need not be true, or even believed to be true. Stereotypes, then, are a much less constrained notion than prototypes. There is, it seems, some danger of the notion of stereotype becoming merely a catch-all notion meaning 'whatever it is we associate with a word that enables us to understand it', unless we can specify in more detail: (1) what kinds of words have stereotypes and (2) what kind of information can appear in stereotypes. In a broad sense, question (2) is easily answered: just about anything, apparently, in the limit. But we should expect that there are at least some regularities to be found here: speculating, we could suggest that some types of word will, for example, have stereotypes largely contaning perceptual information ('lemon'), others might have stereotypes which are primarily functional ('torch'), while still others might have stereotypes which are pretty much all connotation ('spinster').

Before passing on to these questions let us briefly comment on Putnam's 'normal form' for the representation of word meaning, and try to relate it to our earlier suggestions regarding categorial frameworks. A word meaning is represented, for Putnam, by entries under a finite list (a 'vector') of 'syntactic markers', 'semantic markers', 'stereotype' and 'extension'. All the entries except that of extension, says Putnam, are a hypothesis about the individual speaker's competence. Putnam, then, is offering a linguistic theory (he calls it a psycholinguistic theory) about the structural properties of the mental representation of word meaning for a native speaker. The theory claims that this representation contains at least three separable elements each having various features. Presumably Putnam would not want to rule out that there can be a fourth element for many speakers, namely the way to determine the extension, or some quasi-scientific description of the extension, though not necessarily for every speaker, as he has argued. But it is surely just as implausible to maintain that *no* information about extension is ever coded by speakers, as it is to maintain the opposite view. We must make some provision, then, for 'extension'.

A second puzzle concerns the status of Putnam's semantic markers. He is careful to distinguish his use of the term from that of Katz: they are words, 'category indicators of high centrality' (p. 268), not labels for abstract concepts to be found universally, and it is not analytic that a tiger is an animal or that water is liquid. They are, as is suggested by the terminology he uses, the equivalent to what in the terms of our earlier discussion were higher level categories of the relevant categorial framework. But if this is the case, then these semantic markers, for a term like 'water' or 'tiger', at least, must themselves be natural kind terms, although of a higher level of abstraction. 'Animal', 'liquid', etc. describe naturally occurring classes of things presumed to be related via their inner constitution. But that does not seem a correct description for Putnam's other example of a semantic marker, 'natural kind'. This is a metalinguistic term, a term of linguistic theory, singling out a class of words presumed to share certain semantic properties. Earlier, we regarded it as a 'semantic category'.

Like other terms of linguistic theory, or of science in general, it is perhaps plausible to argue that 'natural kind term' itself behaves to a large extent like a natural kind term, in so far as the aim of investigation is to uncover the 'essence' of such semantic or scientific categories. It shares with 'atom', 'quark' and 'molecule' the status of an initially theoretical entity, presumed to correspond to some real phenomenon, whose meaning and extension is not fixed by prior definition, but discovered. But even granting this, there is still a clear distinction to be made between kind terms like 'liquid', and 'natural kind': in particular, it seems reasonable to suppose that the former has a stereotype (free-flowing, takes the shape of its container, etc.) whereas it is difficult to see what the stereotype of 'natural kind' might be. Obviously we ought to distinguish, as we argued above, the type of semantic marker which indicates the higher level category to which the kind belongs (and which licenses the relevant type of inferences as valid), from the type which indicates its 'semantic category'. Putnam is correct to include both in his description, but they are each of a different status: if you understand 'water', you know that it is a liquid, and that it has a certain stereotype. That something may differ from the stereotype and still be water, or fit the stereotype but not be water is also part of your understanding of 'water', but it is not unique to 'water' and is equally true of other natural kind terms. It is just this aspect of knowledge which is captured by assigning 'water' to the semantic category 'natural kind'.

We must extend Putnam's 'vector' to include the following:

(8) < syntactic features, semantic category, address in relevant categorial framework(s) (if any), stereotype, (extension), >

as a 'normal form' for a word meaning. (Perhaps 'stereotype' should be optional, too, for some types of word.) In the case of 'water' its 'address' in the relevant categorial framework tells us that it is a liquid. Its semantic category tells us that 'water is a liquid' is, if true, necessarily true (if 'liquid' is a natural kind, at least) and also that 'water is H_2O' is, if true, necessarily true. There may be more than one entry under 'semantic category', of course: 'water' is also a substance term (as we saw earlier, this is not the same as the syntactic category of 'mass-term'). This entry — if we assume that 'substance term' is also a distinct semantic category — tells us that the sum of any two instances of water is itself water, and so on. Notice that in this vector, both the categorial framework address and the stereotype can change without the extension or reference of the term changing.

We can now turn to the questions raised earlier: how many types of words have stereotypes and, connected to this, what other semantic categories besides 'natural kind word' can be distinguished? Furthermore, do we have a criterion for deciding whether or not something is a natural kind word?

Putnam claims that his theory applies not just to clear cases of natural kind words, but also to 'the great majority of all nouns, and to other parts of speech as well' (p. 242). This is not to suggest that all nouns refer to natural kinds, but that the majority of them share the 'indexical' character of natural kind terms in that they are used with the assumption that the individual referrred to shares the same 'inner constitution', or at least is sufficiently similar to some original or sample members of the category. Verbs like 'grow' and adjectives like 'red', 'all have indexical features' (p. 244). In one passage, he even seems to suggest that words like 'paediatrician', though obviously not singling out a natural kind as such, nevertheless behave like natural kind words in most respects. He goes on to suggest that words like 'pencil' and in general, all words referring to human artefacts are, though not natural kinds, indexical in that they are used intending to refer to whatever has the same 'inner nature' as 'these things here'. This is of course the opposite of the traditional view which has regarded such words as prime examples of analytically definable words.

Putnam, then, is offering his theory as a general theory covering the vast majority of content words of all syntactic categories, even those for which it might seem plausible to postulate analytic definitions. Putnam does concede, as we saw earlier, that there is a category of analytically defined words, or 'one-criterion' words. But he suggests that there is 'a strong tendency for words which are introduced as one-criterion words to develop a natural kind sense, with all the concomitant rigidity and indexicality' (p. 244). Some transformationally derived words (according to Putnam, though of course this is no longer generally believed (Chomsky 1970)) do still retain their one-criterion character: his example is 'hunter': 'one who hunts'. Some syncategorematic words like 'whole' (= every part of) are also one-criterion words, but in general, Putnam seems to be claiming, many plausible looking examples of analyticity will turn out to be natural kind-like terms.

Putnam's claim has not met with universal approval: Schwartz, in two interesting papers (1978, 1980) has taken issue with him and argued that this monolithic approach, assimilating all or most words to a single type, is inadequate: we must make room for a larger class of analytic words, for what he calls, following Locke, 'nominal kinds', that is, any word that is at least partly analytically defined. He gives as examples of these words 'bachelor', 'sloop', 'joke', 'breakfast', 'foreigner' and so on. For these words, some version of the traditional theory, either in the necessary-and-sufficient-properties version or the cluster or family resemblance version is correct, he says, and therefore there are some analytic statements involving them: 'bachelors are unmarried', 'a sloop is a boat', etc. In particular, says Schwartz, names for artefacts are all nominal kinds, not natural kinds and so Putnam's account of words like 'pencil' is inaccurate.

Schwartz's argument is as follows. Putnam's claim that 'pencil' is indexical rests on the claim that we can imagine discovering that pencils were not man-made, but were actually organisms of some kind. It is not too difficult to imagine a plant or tree which secretes graphite into the centre of its stem and grows extremely straight. Let us pretend also that some exotic varieties of this plant even grow in a hexagonal shape and have strange markings that look like '2B' or 'Venus' or 'Government Property' on the side. All you do to get a pencil is harvest them, sharpen them up and possibly put a rubber on one end. This is, as before, pretty implausible, but it is consistent and conceivable in the sense that round squares are not conceivable. The point of this thought experiment as with the earlier ones is that if you can imagine these organisms still being called 'pencils', then 'pencils are artefacts' cannot be analytic. Schwartz so far agrees with Putnam that all this is so. But he says that Putnam is wrong to infer from this that 'pencil' is indexical, for all that strictly follows is that the term 'artefact' is not analytically connected to 'pencil'. However, it does not follow from this fact that there are no other analytic statements involving 'pencil'. And if there are, then 'pencil' is a nominal kind term, not a natural kind term. Schwartz claims, without going into detail, that 'pencil' is analytically defined in terms of its extension having a particular function and form: all pencils have a certain function and form, and anything that has that function and form is a pencil.

Schwartz is proposing, then, that the semantic category 'natural kind term' is not as all-inclusive as Putnam has claimed, but that there is also a semantic category of 'nominal kind term': words that have an 'analytic specification'. Schwartz seems to intend 'analytic specification' to be understood in the strong sense of something which provides necessary and sufficient conditions for membership of the extension (1980:182, though see 1978:572 fn.12). This view seems to challenge the position arrived at in an earlier chapter, where we argued that there were in fact very few examples of fully satisfactory definitions of meanings of words. However, as was made clear there, this is not the same as claiming that there are no analytic relations between words, for there seemed to be some cases where there were entailments from a word, but that this entailment relation was one way only, not two ways, as the strong analytic thesis would claim. The question then arose as to how it was possible to understand words of this type. Whereas on the strong analytic thesis – that the relation between word and definition is biconditional – the claim that a word is analytically definable provides us with an account of how we are able to understand that word (assuming we understand the definition), on the weaker analytic thesis – that the definition provides only a necessary condition, not also a sufficient one – we have to explain how we can understand that word when the definition may not be sufficient to distinguish it from other closely related words. (For example, if a 'pencil' is a 'thing for writing with', how do we distinguish 'pen' from 'pencil'?)

However, for both the weak and the strong thesis we can distinguish between two kinds of semantic associations: first, what we will call 'reductive' specifications, on which the meaning of a term is (perhaps only partly) specified in terms of other, independently understood terms; and, secondly, 'non-reductive' specifications, in which the meaning is given by means of other terms which may appear prima facie to be different, but which turn out ultimately to presuppose an understanding of the term being defined (examples like Molière's 'dormitive potency' definition illustrate the kind of thing meant here). We are entitled to require, I think, that as an explanation of our understanding of a term, an analytic specification should be a reductive one: a non-reductive one might be a true statement about the meaning of the word, but it cannot be intended as a claim about our understanding of it, for it ultimately turns out to presuppose that understanding. Notice that if an analytic specification involved natural kind terms, this would count as a reductive specification, for it describes our understanding of the term at least partly in terms of words the understanding of which is independently accounted for.

In order, then, to admit 'nominal kind term' as a separate semantic category, we need to ask: (1) Are the definitions for the words in question reductive? (2) Are they strongly or weakly analytic? (3) If the latter, what else needs to be added to explain our understanding of them?

Schwartz proposes a general criterion (which we in fact drew on earlier) for distinguishing natural and nominal kind words in terms of what he calls a 'stable generalisation'. This involves the notions of 'corrigibility' and of the 'counter-example test'. If you ask of a sentence like 'dogs are animals', 'Could (all) dogs have turned out not to be animals?' and the answer is 'yes' then the statement that dogs are animals is corrigible and therefore not analytic. If you then ask, 'given that we think dogs are animals, could the 1,000th dog not be an animal when the other 999 were?' and the answer is 'no', then the statement has also passed the counter-example test — it is not refutable by a lone counter-example (though, as we said, with a significant number we would be less sure). It is thus metaphysically or linguistically necessary. Statements which are both corrigible and pass the counter-example test are stable generalisations. They are statements reflecting our most fundamental beliefs about the structure of the world, as reflected in categorial frameworks involving natural kinds. Schwartz's criterion for natural kind terms is this: something is a natural kind term if and only if it figures as the subject term in some stable generalisation. Something is a nominal kind term if and only if it does *not* figure in any stable generalisation. Statements involving nominal kind terms — 'circles are round' — will either be analytic, or straightforwardly contingent — 'circles are difficult to draw'.

It follows from this criterion, says Schwartz, that no natural kind term can figure in the analytic specification of a nominal kind term.

For if it did, that specification would entail any statement where the natural kind term was replaced by a coextensive or entailed term. For example, take a purportedly analytic statement like:

(9) Boats are intended for use on water

Since water is H_2O,

(10) Boats are intended for use on H_2O

will also be true. But (10) is corrigible, since water might not have been H_2O. If water is H_2O, however, then it is H_2O necessarily, so (10) passes the counter-example test and is a stable generalisation. So 'boat', by the criterion, is a natural kind term and we have derived a contradiction of our original hypothesis that 'boat' was analytically specified.

Schwartz's second example is 'bachelor'. Consider these sentences:

(11) Bachelors are adult male humans who have never married
(12) Humans are animals
(13) Bachelors are animals

From (11) and (12) we can infer (13), which seems to be corrigible, in the sense that humans might have turned out not to be included in the category 'animal', and stable, in that given that they haven't, we can't imagine a non-animal human or, therefore, a non-animal bachelor. So 'bachelor' is a natural kind, by the criterion, and we have a contradiction again, apparently at least. Schwartz argues from his criterion that the properties associated with a nominal kind must be either analytic or contingent; since assuming that they are analytic leads to a contradiction, we must conclude instead that 'boats are used on water' and 'bachelors are human beings' are contingent. For example, we could use boats on lakes of milk or even dust, but they would still be boats. That bachelors are human beings is (perhaps less clearly) contingent: a race of reptile humanoids with similar marriage customs could also have bachelors, Schwartz thinks. Similar arguments can be brought forward for the appearance of natural kinds in other supposedly analytic specifications, and so they all must be contingent.

If Schwartz is correct, then it is going to be rather difficult to find analytic definitions of nominal kind terms that are reductive in the sense just discussed. For although it may be that there are analytic definitions, these will be couched in terms of words which are not natural kind terms. Unless there is some third category of word involved, this means that they must themselves be nominal kind terms. This raises a picture of an interlocking system of nominal kind terms each defined in terms of other nominal kind terms. But then the question is: how do we understand these definitions? At least one group of definitions must make contact with something outside of this system, break out of the circle, for otherwise the process of understanding would be an impossible bootstrapping operation. One possibility, perhaps, if natural kind terms are not involved, is that there is some primitive element of ostension, or 'indexicality' involved in the definition of at least some nominal kinds. But even this is not the case, according to Schwartz: nominal kind terms are all non-indexical (1980:184).

Fortunately, we can show that the two supposed implications of Schwartz's criterion, namely: (i) natural kinds do not appear in analytic specifications; and (ii) analytic specifications of nominal kinds do not involve indexicality do not hold, and so we are not faced with the awkward dichotomy of vocabulary just suggested. To begin with, let us notice that Schwartz's first argument, about 'boat', is formally invalid. 'Intend' creates an opaque context, and so the most that can be inferred from 'boats are intended for use on water' and 'water is H_2O' is

(14) The stuff that boats are intended for use on is H_2O

which is certainly corrigible, and a stable generalisation; but it is a stable generalisation about water, not about boats. So we do not derive any contradiction here.

Let us go back to 'pencil'. If Schwartz is correct, then there should be some properties analytically connected with it (though these will not include being an artefact). Schwartz suggests that form and function are general defining properties for artefacts. If this is true then we ought to be able to find some analytic description of a pencil's form and/or function. Schwartz does not give one, but if he is correct it should be possible to come up with something. One possible candidate is in fact suggested (and dismissed) by Putnam. He says that it is commonly (and he implies, wrongly) thought that 'standardly intended to be written with' is analytically connected with 'pencil'. Let us take this as a starting point. It is correct I think that this particular functional property is not analytically tied to 'pencil'. Certainly, all pencils are currently intended to be written with. But it is easy to imagine pencils becoming so thoroughly superseded that they are never used for writing, even though people continue to manufacture them as curios or ornaments.

They might even be manufactured in greater numbers than before (consider horse brasses or flintlock pistols here). What is the case, however, is that pencils must be *capable* of being written with, a similar but different property. However much we vary the form of these ornamental pencils, if they are not in principle capable of being written with, they are not real pencils: we would have to call them toy or imitation pencils. Likewise with flintlocks: a pistol that can't fire is an imitation pistol, not a real pistol. It is then false that artefacts are defined in terms of what they are standardly intended for, for that could change quite drastically: what is important is whether they can still do what they were originally intended for.

Thus we have a candidate for a necessary property for 'pencil'; they must be capable of being written with. Is it a sufficient one? Clearly not: a pencil is not distinguished from pens, crayons, chalk or charcoal or many other items by this criterion. I would suggest that we need at least the further requirements that the function be carried out by leaving a solid dry deposit (rather than a liquid or glycerine deposit, ruling out pens and ballpoints) and that the medium by which this is achieved be encased in some way, ruling out chalk and charcoal. (Even this will not capture eyebrow pencil or light pencil: but there are two reasons why this should not worry us: (a) they need their qualifying noun, (b) they could equally aptly be called pens.) If this is accurate then we have a necessary and possibly even sufficient analytic definition,[3] though given the discussion of Chapter 2 we should not be too sanguine about this.

Now if Schwartz's criterion is correct, all the properties of 'pencil' should either be contingent, or analytic; and the latter properties will not contain any natural kind words. Let us assume that the following is a comprehensive list:

(i) Pencils are artefacts
(ii) Made of graphite
(iii) Usually encased in wood
(iv) Shaped thus: (imagine your favourite pencil)
(v) They can be used to make marks with
(vi) By leaving a solid dry deposit on some surface
(vii) The medium accomplishing (vi) must be encased

We have already established that (i) is not analytic, and (ii) and (iii) clearly are also contingent: new materials for the construction of pencils may be just round the corner. And although (iv) is not wholly contingent, in the sense that function imposes some limits on form, it is not wholly analytic either. (v), (vi) and (vii) are analytic, we are claiming, and therefore not corrigible: (ii)-(iv) are corrigible but they do not pass the counter-example test.

But there is a strong prima facie case for claiming that at least two of the terms appearing in the analytic specification (vi) are natural kind words, namely 'solid' and 'dry'. Words like 'solid' and 'liquid' are complicated of course, because they have both an everyday sense and a fairly technical scientific sense. Let us concentrate first of all on the scientific sense of 'solid': in this sense, there are actually, I gather, three kinds of solid: crystals, polymers and glasses. While in many other respects they differ, they all count as being solids because their molecules are, in comparison with liquids or gases, in a low state of agitation. Now, in unclear cases, this could be made into a defining feature: if for some substance it was unclear whether it was solid or liquid, then some threshold of molecular agitation could be specified at which anything falling under it would be a solid. So this could be an analytic specification and so 'solid' would be a nominal kind term. But by this token, so could any property: we could choose to make it criterial for difficult cases. If we discount this possibility as irrelevant, therefore, it becomes clear that the statement that 'solid things have molecules in a low state of agitation' is, like any other scientific discovery, corrigible: we could have discovered that what made solid things solid was having sticky molecules, molecules with hooks on, or something like that. But it is also clear that given that 999 solid things are solid for this reason, then we cannot really imagine the 1,000th thing being solid for a completely different reason. The situation is identical to that described by Kripke for statements like 'gold has atomic number 79': or 'heat is the motion of molecules': if they are true at all, then these theoretical identifications are true necessarily. But this means that the above statement is a stable generalisation and 'solid' is therefore a natural kind term, by Schwartz's criterion.

Although this seems correct, there is nevertheless a good counterargument that 'solid', 'dry', etc. do at least partly have analytic specifications and so cannot, if Schwartz is right, be genuine natural kind terms. A solid object might be defined, for example, as an object which, relatively speaking, resists penetration. A dry object is presumably one which contains no liquid. It certainly seems to be true that it is impossible to imagine solid or dry objects without these properties. But notice that these specifications are all of the non-reductive kind: the concepts involved turn out, on reflection, to presuppose one another.

'Resist' and 'penetration' are already implicitly using the notion of solidity: 'resistance' is the force one solid object exerts upon contact with another; it is impossible to 'penetrate' something that offers no resistance. Similarly with 'dry', 'wet' and 'liquid': 'dry', let us say, is defined in terms of not being wet, or not containing liquid. How is 'wet' defined? Presumably in terms of 'liquid'. How is 'liquid' defined? Perhaps (non-scientifically) something which takes the shape of its container: but how can *this* notion be described without invoking solidity, or resistance?

Observations about the interconnectedness of these terms are not new, of course: essentially the same point can be found in Locke (Ch. 4, Book II, p. 103). More recently Bennett (1971:97) has pointed out the interdependence of these concepts with those like shape and size. These seem to form a network of conceptual connections which come all of a piece, as it were: it does not seem possible to isolate any of them as more basic than the others.

But we now have something of a problem, for words like these we are discussing seem to be some kind of hybrid, having features of both natural and nominal kind words but not falling completely into either category. The simplest answer to this problem is to claim that in fact they are members of a third and separate semantic category, which with a gesture towards Locke we can call the category of 'primary kind' words. These include words like 'solid', 'dry', 'liquid', 'hot', 'yellow', 'soft', 'smooth' and such like. Although most of these words are primarily adjectives, they can also appear as nouns.

Of course, having claimed the existence of a third semantic category, it is now incumbent on us to provide some criteria which will distinguish its members from members of the other categories. In particular, since we have claimed that the analytic specifications associated with primary kind words are non-reductive it follows that our understanding of such concepts cannot come ultimately from these non-reductive analytic specifications but from some other source. At some point this semantic circle must be broken and refer to something independently understood. Does our understanding then perhaps come via the reference of these terms, in the same way as for 'gold' or 'tiger', or other natural kinds?

If this is taken to mean 'does our understanding of these terms proceed in exactly the same way as for these other standard examples', the answer must be 'no'. 'Solid' and 'liquid', although by Schwartz's criterion they count as natural kind words, nevertheless behave differently in at least two respects from our earlier examples of natural kinds. Take 'gold', for example. While we might turn out to have been mistaken about the superficial features of gold (yellow, heavy, malleable) that we used to fix the referent, and although superficial features may mislead us in the case of particular samples, nevertheless as long as something has the essential properties or inner constitution (atomic number 79) of gold it will actually be gold. If it has a different atomic number it will be a different substance, however many of the superficial features it possesses. More generally, for these natural kinds, having the essential properties they have is constitutive of a distinct natural kind; having the superficial properties generally is not. But neither of these is true for 'solid' and 'liquid': while having relatively motionless and relatively agitated molecules is an essential property of a solid or a liquid, if something loses this property it does not thereby become a different substance: water can be ice, steam or liquid and there is no urge to say that solid H_2O is a different *substance* from liquid H_2O. Thus the essential properties of such terms are not constitutive of different kinds but of particular states of kinds. They cross-classify other kinds.

And the superficial features of these terms also play a different role. Although in the case of 'gold' and 'tiger' etc. we could turn out to be wrong about the superficial features by which we fix their reference, in the case of 'solid' and 'liquid', 'dry' and 'wet', etc. we could not. We can be wrong about particular applications of the terms – mistakes, illusions, hallucinations, etc. ('it felt solid at first, but then I pushed my fingers through and it melted away') – but it couldn't turn out that *all* solid things did not resist penetration, that wet things did not feel like *that*, that all liquid things should turn out not to take the shape of their container, and so on. This does not mean that such statements are analytic in the required, reductive sense (even if they might be analytic in the non-reductive sense), but it does mean that they are incorrigible in a way that 'gold is yellow', 'tigers are striped', and so on are not incorrigible. So these terms are quite thoroughly indexical: to be solid is to feel like *that*: and in the everyday sense of 'solid', feeling solid is just to be solid.

Many others of these adjectives behave in a similar way: colour words for example. We can conceive of different kinds of explanations for colour; we can even accept that our naïve belief that colour is a property of objects is wrong (if we are shown them in a different coloured light, or learn about the physiology of perception) but we cannot imagine 'yellow' not being *that* colour there (though obviously we could imagine it being called something else). We can summarise this property of primary kind terms by reference to their stereotype: if these observations are correct then at least one property mentioned in the stereotype of such a term is analytically connected to that term; though it is the fact that it is in the stereotype rather than that it is analytically connected that is important for our understanding of the term.

Neither of the alleged implications of Schwartz's criterion then turns out to be true: words having some of the properties of natural kind words figure in the specification of nominal kind words, and nominal kind words inherit a measure of indexicality through this. It is in fact difficult to see how things could be otherwise, for if Schwartz was correct, as remarked, it would seem to imply a strict dichotomy of all words between natural and nominal kinds, the two types not interacting. But then it is difficult to see how an analytic specification of a nominal kind could ever be reductive, as it needs to be if it is to stand as an account of how we understand it.

IV

It is clear that in order to do justice to these facts and to our earlier observations about 'pencil', Schwartz's criterion for distinguishing nominal and natural kind terms must be amended. As it stood, incidentally, it was in any case inadequate, for it takes natural kind terms as basic, defined in terms of appearance in stable generalisations; defining nominal kind terms, in effect, as whatever is not a natural kind term by this criterion. But this is far too loose, for by such a criterion a word which has associated with it *only* properties which were loosely contingent — properties which were sufficient, but not necessary, and easily imaginable as lacking — would count trivially as a nominal kind term. All the semantic statements with such a term as subject would be corrigible, but they would fail the counter-example test. This does not seem very satisfactory, as no candidates for such a word readily spring to mind and there are good prima facie reasons for saying that this is an impossible type of word in a natural language (what could it be used for?).

Let us begin with nominal kinds. We have seen that there are some nominal kinds which include primary kinds in their analytic specification. Are there in fact any examples of nominal kind words which do not behave in this way, as Schwartz originally envisaged? It seems to me that though many words on analysis may be found to contain implicit reference to some primary or even some natural kind, we can nevertheless distinguish those for which this implicit reference is not crucial:

examples like 'bachelor', as discussed earlier, might fall into this category: other candidates might be words like 'policeman' or 'paediatrician'. As things stand these terms presently refer to human beings, which we assume to be a natural kind, but it is not logically inconsistent to imagine a non-human society in which some individuals performed analogous roles, and it seems plausible that we might then refer to them as policemen or paediatricians. But what does not seem possible to imagine is that in that society a 'policeman' was someone who was not employed to uphold the law, or that a 'paediatrician' was not a doctor specialising in treating the young of the species. These seem to be genuinely analytic connections, and to be somehow a more important aspect of the meanings of these terms than the component which can be related to natural or to primary kind words.

Furthermore, in trying to take natural kind terms as basic, Schwartz has already presupposed the only notion he needs to define nominal kinds: the notion of incorrigibility. For when we examine his criterion it is clear that 'incorrigible' is effectively a synonym for *analytic* and/or *a priori*, since metaphysically necessary truths are corrigible. It would be much simpler then to define a nominal kind term as anything which figures as subject term in some (reductive) analytic specification. (A reductive analytic specification is an analytic connection of the type defined in Chapter 2.) A natural kind term is one which figures as subject of a stable generalisation. No natural kind terms are the subjects of analytic specifications (unless we count primary kinds as a subset of natural kinds rather than as a separate category). But some nominal kinds seem to figure as the subjects of stable generalisations, as was the case above for 'bachelor' and 'policeman', where these stable generalisations are, as it were, spurious: not important or central to the meaning of the term. (This may be the kind of thing Putnam had in mind when he talked about one-criterion words developing indexicality.)

Notice that a primary kind term figures both as subject of some stable generalisation (in all the examples given, this will be a fairly technical statement) and as subject of a non-reductive analytic statement. Since it is a non-reductive statement, though, it cannot be via such specifications that we come to understand all such terms (though given the understanding of some, we could arrive at the others which are defined in terms of them). It is the stereotype — which will be difficult to describe in words, often — which we associate with these terms that provides our understanding of them. Whereas the stereotype associated with a natural kind term can change without there necessarily being an associated change of meaning, the stereotype of a primary kind term could not change in this way: the way solid things feel, or the way yellow things look could not come to be associated with other terms without making them synonymous with 'yellow' or 'solid'. We could, then, describe the difference between primary and natural kind terms in this way instead. The stereotype of a natural kind term can change, whereas the stereotype of a primary kind term cannot.

But do we not now have the kind of contradiction that Schwartz was concerned to avoid? If (a) some nominal kinds figure in stable generalisations, as they seem to, won't they also qualify as natural kinds? And if (b) some nominal kinds contain a reference to primary kinds in their analytic specification, won't we again be able to infer some stable generalisation from this, leading once more to a contradiction?

The answer to this is no. There is a deeper generalisation underlying both (a) and (b), the existence of which undermines Schwartz's arguments that such occurrences lead to contradictions. For if some nominal kind mentions a primary or a natural kind in its specification, invariably the reference is to the superficial features of the kind that the terms of the specification refer to, those which are reference-fixing for it, rather than those which are essential to it. We can again state this in terms of 'stereotype':

(15) Reference to a natural or primary kind within an analytic specification is to its stereotype, not to its essential properties

If it is part of the meaning of 'boat' that it is intended for use on water, what is meant by that is that it is for use on something having the relevant superficial properties of water: offering buoyancy, easy penetrability, etc. — not to something having the essential properties of water. As we saw, we could have boats on seas of milk, beer or even dust: but we could not have boats on seas of hard concrete. The actual inner constitution of the medium is irrelevant, but the superficial properties must be sufficiently like water. Likewise, if it is part of the analytic specification of 'bachelor' that bachelors are human, what is meant by that is that it is only the external properties of human beings that are relevant to the meaning of 'bachelor': their social institutions, legal practices, domestic customs, and so on. Any collection of some other kinds of creature (or machines, presumably) in which similar social structures could be identified could contain bachelors, just as boats could float on dust. But bachelors of whatever species who are married, or boats that do not float on whatever medium has the superficial features of water, are not real bachelors and not real boats.

The generalisation that analytic specifications only involve superficial features or stereotypes of course also embraces the occurrence of primary kinds in them, for which superficial features are, in a sense, all there is. Notice that if we try to deduce stable generalisations akin to the examples like 'boats are for use on H_2O' the effect is even more ludicrous: 'pencils leave a deposit whose molecules are in a relatively low state of agitation'. In both cases the bizarreness of the generalisation is due to the fact that we have moved from features of the stereotype of the term, which are important for the definition, to features from the description of the extension of the term, which are not. Although they may be true, these generalisations are incidental to the meaning of the term. In fact, even if they turned out to be false, the meaning of the term would not change, if the generalisation stated in (15) is correct. If water turned out to be XYZ and not H_2O, it would still be true that boats were vehicles which used water as their medium. All that is important is the superficial nature: what water actually *is* is irrelevant to an understanding of 'boat'. Thus the fact that a nominal kind term may figure in some stable generalisation does not matter once we realise that they are irrelevant to its meaning. These spurious stable generalisations must be distinguished from those concerning the reference of natural kind terms; once this is done we avoid Schwartz's contradiction.

We have assumed tentatively that the analytic specification for 'pencil' in terms of form and function constituted both necessary and sufficient conditions for something being a pencil. However, the vast majority of analytic specifications seem to be conditional only, not biconditional (if something is an X, then . . .), as we discussed in an earlier chapter. We must then settle a question raised again a few pages ago: if these analytic specifications are conditional only, how do we keep items which may have the same analytic specification apart? For example, it seems likely that 'glass' and 'goblet' could largely coincide in an analytic specification of their form and function. If the analytic specification in these terms is all there is to their meaning, why are they not regarded as synonymous with each other?

The answer is surely that we have different stereotypes for each of these: it is not analytic, let us assume, that glasses and goblets have exactly the shape that they do, for we could imagine other possibilities, but the typical glass has such and such a shape and is a familiar domestic item, whereas a goblet has another sort of shape and is altogether a much more elevated vessel. Stereotypes will usually contain information about the appearance of the item, at least, but we might also include aspects that would normally be regarded as connotations, such as the information that goblets are usually used on special occasions or in grand circumstances.

Where the analytic specification of an artefact term via its form and function is not a biconditional, all sorts of objects might be as it were 'accidentally' capable of satisfying it. If the definition is correct, then we ought to be able to envisage the term being used of it quasi-metaphorically: this seems to be the case, when we consider the range of objects that can (and cannot) be pressed into service as a boat, a hammer or a table. We know what a typical hammer looks like, though we also know that a brick can be used as a hammer. We know what a typical table looks like, but we will also accept that the weird looking object that we are sitting at is nevertheless a table. During the summer when news is slack our papers regularly report some eccentric sailor being rescued from a home-made 'boat' that used to be an oildrum or an old pram. But although they might be able to fulfil the relevant function in the requisite manner these objects fail to satisfy the stereotype associated with the term and so they are not regarded as genuine instances. If there were not this extra factor over and above the analytic specification it would be difficult to explain why we did not apply the term literally to objects under these circumstances.

It seems to me that the assumption that nominal kinds also have stereotypes is a natural way of accounting for this range of intuitions. Nevertheless, it is still the case that in some sense, the stereotype associated with a nominal kind term, where there is one — we are not claiming that all nominal kind terms have stereotypes — is somehow a less important part of its meaning than it is for a natural or a primary kind term. The analytic specification alone, when it is only conditional, may not be sufficient to use the term fully appropriately, but it is crucial to an understanding of the term in a way in which the (non-reductive) analytic specifications associated with primary kind terms are not. For these, as for natural kind terms, it is the stereotype that counts.

Using the relative importance of stereotypes as a third parameter, then, we can produce a final summary of the similarities and differences between the three semantic categories that we have been discussing in this chapter, as follows:

168 *Semantic categories*

	Subject of some stable generalisation	Subject of some analytic specification	Understood primarily via stereotype
Natural	√	X	√
Nominal	can be	√	X
Primary	√	can be	√

This does not provide an exhaustive account of their semantic properties but is a useful way of comparing them, and provided that the parameters we are using are satisfactory, means that we have achieved our original objective of providing criteria for distinguishing between these three categories.

V

While these are modest beginnings, I hope that this chapter has shown that it is possible to isolate semantic categories and to say something revealing about their nature and their interaction with each other. Of course, it is unlikely that even in the relatively limited domains we have looked at, the particular three categories just discussed will cover every possibility exhaustively, and when we look at, say, verbs and adverbs, it is clear that there is much work left to do.

These definitions of semantic categories, as well as generalisations like that expressed by (15), and the principles of nameability and of categorisation discussed in earlier chapters, are intended as a contribution to a theory of word meaning which bears the same relation to the lexicon of an individual language as does the theory of universal grammar to the grammar of an individual language: in fact, on the wider interpretation of 'grammar' it is intended as a contribution to universal grammar. That is to say, it provides what is assumed to be common to all languages; principles of nameability, categorisation, criteria for analyticity, natural, nominal and primary kind term, and so on, whereas the individual lexicon will reflect in large part culture and language specific information. Nevertheless, reference to both is necessary for a complete account of the ability of the native speaker.

It is not just in elaborating semantic categories that other domains have much still to yield. For example, there are many parallels between verbs and nouns which lead us to expect that we might find there some parallels to the principles of nameability sketched in Chapter 3. Several authors have pointed out that there is a semantic parallel between verbs which refer to events, and count nouns, on the one hand, and between verbs which refer to processes, and substance nouns, on the other (see Mourelatos 1978 for a review and discussion). It seems quite likely, therefore, that something akin to the nameability principles is at work there also, determining what counts as a 'naturally nameable event'. Further, we might explore the hypothesis that verbs depend partly for their interpretations on categorial frameworks which are more abstract and elaborated than the ones we have discussed here, perhaps consisting of almost entirely covert categories of 'agent', 'action', 'instrument', 'state' and such like, related not by inclusion or membership but by principles or axioms of a system of 'commonsense' or 'practical' reasoning involving volitions, intentions, results, causes and other abstract ontological categories and relations. Making such hypotheses precise enough to be tested will be a challenging business, but if this enterprise should prove at all successful it would be an interesting and worthwhile justification of the approach begun in a small way here.

Notes

1. See Schwartz (ed.) (1977) and references there for a fuller account, and a critical exposition.
2. Chomsky elsewhere (1980:62) describes these sorts of intuitions as 'dubious'. I find this rather surprising: notwithstanding his alleged counter-example, it seems to me that when misunderstandings about exactly what one is being asked to imagine are cleared up, our intuitions are on the whole quite straightforward. 'Cats are animals' could have turned out to be false, but hasn't: 'circles are round' could not turn out to be false.
3. 'Pencil' is analytically defined in terms of its function, where this has to be carried out in a certain manner. Naturally, these requirements impose restraints on the form which a pencil can have (a pencil where the point is doubled back half way along its length cannot be written with, for example). We might maintain that for nouns describing human artefacts this was generally the case: they are defined in terms of capability of fulfilling a particular function in a particular manner. This certainly seems to be true of our other example, 'boat', which can br provisionally analysed (see below) as 'a vehicle capable of transport over a medium having the relevant superficial properties of water'. This will include ornamental or toy boats only to the extent that they are capable of fulfilling this function, in the required manner, and the form of boats will be constrained likewise. We might propose, therefore, that the general form of analytic specification for words for human artefacts will be 'capable of fulfilling function F in manner M'.

BIBLIOGRAPHY

Where a work is cited as being reprinted in a collection, page references in the text are to that version.

Anderson, E.S. (1978) 'Lexical Universals of Body-Part Terminology' in Greenberg, Ferguson and Moravscik (1978)
Anderson, S.R. and Kiparsky, P. (eds.) (1973) *A Festschrift for Morris Halle*, New York: Holt, Rinehart and Winston
Anglin, J.M. (1977) *Word, Object and Conceptual Development*, New York: Norton
Austin, J.L. (1961) 'The Meaning of a Word' in J.L. Austin, *Philosophical Papers*, London: Oxford University Press (2nd edn 1970)
Basso, K.H. (1968) 'The Western Apache Classificatory Verb System: A Formal Analysis', *Southwestern Journal of Anthropology*, 24, 252-66
Battig, W.F. and Montague, W.E. (1969) 'Category Norms for Verbal Items in 56 Categories: A Replication and Extension of the Connecticut Category Norms', *Journal of Experimental Psychology*, 80 (Monograph Supplement 3, pt. 2)
Benacerraf, P. and Putnam, H. (eds.) (1964) *Philosophy of Mathematics: Selected Readings*, Englewood Cliffs, NJ: Prentice-Hall Inc.
Bendix, E.H. (1966) *Componential Analysis of General Vocabulary: The Semantic Structure of a Set of Verbs in English, Hindi and Japanese*, The Hague: Mouton Publishers
Bennett, J. (1971) *Locke, Berkeley, Hume: Central Themes*, Oxford: Clarendon Press
Berlin, B. (1978) 'Ethnobiological Classification' in Rosch and Lloyd (1978)
Berlin, B., Breedlove, D. and Raven, P. (1968) 'Covert Categories and Folk Taxonomies', *American Anthropologist*, 70, 290-9
— (1975) 'General Principles of Classification and Nomenclature in Folk Biology', *American Anthropologist*, 75, 214-42
Berlin, B. and Kay, P. (1969) *Basic Color Terms*, Berkeley: University of California Press
Bever, T.G. and Rosenbaum, P.S. (1971) 'Some Lexical Structures and Their Empirical Validity' in Steinberg and Jacobovits (1971)

Bierwisch, M. (1971) 'On Classifying Semantic Features' in Steinberg and Jacobovits (1971)

Binnick, R. (1972) '"Will" and "be going to" II' in Peranteau *et al.*, (1972)

Bolinger, D. (1965) 'The Atomisation of Meaning', *Language, 41*, 555-73

Bower, T.G.R. (1974) *Development in Infancy*, San Francisco: Freeman

— (1977)*The Perceptual World of the Child*, London: Fontana

— (1979) *Human Development*, San Francisco: Freeman

Bowerman, M. (1977) 'The Acquisition of Word Meaning' in P. Johnson-Laird and P. Wason (eds.), *Thinking*, Cambridge: Cambridge University Press

Carterette, E.C. and Friedman, M.P. (eds.) (1978) *Perceptual Processing*, New York: Academic Press

Chomsky, N. (1959) 'A review of B.F. Skinner's "Verbal Behaviour"', in Fodor and Katz (1964)

— (1965) *Aspects of the Theory of Syntax*, Cambridge, Mass.: MIT Press

— (1969) 'Quine's Empirical Assumptions' in Davidson and Hintikka (1969)

— (1970) 'Remarks on Nominalisations' in R.A. Jacobs and P.S. Rosenbaum (eds.), *Readings in English Transformational Grammar*, Waltham, Mass.: Ginn & Co.

— (1971) 'Deep Structure, Surface Structure, and Semantic Interpretation' in Steinberg and Jacobovits (1971)

— (1976) *Reflections on Language*, London: Temple Smith

— (1980) *Rules and Representations*, Oxford: Basil Blackwell

Clark, H.H. and Clark, E.V. (1977) *Psychology and Language: An Introduction to Psycholinguistics*, New York: Harcourt Brace Jovanovich Inc.

Cole, P. and Morgan, J. (eds.) (1975) *Syntax and Semantics Vol. III: Speech Acts*, New York: Academic Press

Coleman, L. and Kay, P. (1981) 'Prototype Semantics: The English Word "Lie"' *Language, 57*, 26-44

Cruse, D.A. (1979) 'On the Transitivity of the Part-whole Relation', *Journal of Linguistics, 15*, 29-38

Darden, B.J., Bailey, C.J.N. and Davison, A. (eds.) (1968) *Papers from the 4th Regional Meeting of the Chicago Linguistics Society*, University of Chicago: Department of Linguistics

Davidson, D. (1967a) 'The Logical Form of Action Sentences' in

N. Rescher (ed.), *The Logic of Decision and Action*, Pittsburgh: University of Pittsburgh Press
— (1967b) 'Truth and Meaning', *Synthese, 17*, 304-23
— (1969) 'On Saying That' in Davidson and Hintikka (1969)
— (1973) 'Radical Interpretation', *Dialectica, 27*, 313-28
— (1974a) 'Belief and the Basis of Meaning', *Synthese, 27*, 309-23
— (1974b) 'Psychology as Philosophy' in S.C. Brown (ed.), *The Philosophy of Psychology*, London: Macmillan. Reprinted in Davidson (1980)
— (1980) *Essays on Actions and Events*, Oxford: Clarendon Press
Davidson, D. and Harman, G. (eds.) (1972) *Semantics of Natural Language*, Dordrecht: Reidel Publishing Co.
Davidson, D. and Hintikka, K.J.J. (eds.) (1969) *Words and Objections: Essays on the Work of W.V. Quine*, Dordrecht: Reidel Publishing Co.
Davis, J.W. et al., (1969) *Philosophical Logic*, Dordrecht: Reidel Publishing Co.
Dixon, R.M.W. (1971) 'A Method of Semantic Description' in Steinberg and Jacobovits (1971)
Donnellan, K. (1966) 'Reference and Definite Descriptions', *Philosophical Review, LXXV*, 281-304. Reprinted in Steinberg and Jacobovits (1971)
Dowty, D. (1979) *Word Meaning in Montague Grammar*, Dordrecht: Reidel Publishing Co.
Evans, G. and McDowell, J. (eds.) (1976) *Truth and Meaning*, Oxford: Oxford University Press
Fillmore, C.J. (1971) 'Verbs of Judging: An Exercise in Semantic Description' in C.J. Fillmore and D.T. Langendoen (eds.) *Studies in Linguistic Semantics*, New York: Holt, Rinehart & Winston
Fodor, J.A. (1968) *Psychological Explanation: An Introduction to the Philosophy of Psychology*, New York: Random House
— (1970) 'Three Reasons for Not Deriving "Kill" from "Cause to Die"', *Linguistic Inquiry, 1.4*, 429-38
— (1972) 'Troubles about Actions' in Davidson and Harman (1972)
— (1975) *The Language of Thought*, Hassocks, Sussex: The Harvester Press
Fodor, J.A., Bever, T.G. and Garrett, M.F. (1974) *The Psychology of Language: An Introduction to Psycholinguistics and Generative Grammar*, New York: McGraw-Hill
Fodor, J.A. and Katz, J.J. (1964) *The Structure of Language: Readings in the Philosophy of Language*, Englewood Cliffs, NJ: Prentice-Hall Inc.

Fodor, J.A. *et. al.* (1980) 'Against Definitions', *Cognition, 8*, 263-367

Fodor, J.D. (1977) *Semantics: Theories of Meaning in Generative Grammar*, Hassocks, Sussex: The Harvester Press

Foster, J.A. (1976) 'Meaning and Truth Theory', in Evans and McDowell (1976)

Geach, P. (1957) *Mental Acts: Their Content and Their Objects*, London: Routledge and Kegan Paul

Gibson, R.F. Jr (1980) 'Are There Really Two Quines?', *Erkenntnis, 15*, 349-70

Goodman, N. (1951) *The Structure of Appearance*, Cambridge, Mass.: Harvard University Press

Greenberg, J.H, Ferguson, C.H. and Moravscik, E.A. (eds.) (1978) *Universals of Human Language, Vol. 3, Word Structure*, Stanford: Stanford University Press

Grice, H.P. (1975) 'Logic and Conversation' in Cole and Morgan (1975)

Grice, H.P. and Strawson, P.F. (1956) 'In Defense of a Dogma', *Philosophical Review*, 66. Reprinted in Rosenberg and Travis (1971)

Gunderson, K. and Maxwell, G. (eds.) (1975) *Minnesota Studies in Philosophy of Science Vol. 6*, Minneapolis: University of Minnesota Press

Harris, Z. (1951) *Methods in Structural Linguistics*, Chicago: University of Chicago Press. Reprinted as *Structural Linguistics* (1961)

Hayes, P.J. (1978) 'The Naive Physics Manifesto', mimeo: Dept. of Computer Science, University of Essex

Hays, W. (1963) *Statistics for Psychologists*, New York: Holt, Rinehart & Winston

Hockney, D. (1975) 'The Bifurcation of Scientific Theories and the Indeterminacy of Translation', *Philosophy of Science, 42*, 411-27

Jackendoff, R. (1976) 'Toward an Explanatory Semantic Representation', *Linguistic Inquiry, 7.1*, 89-150

Katz, J.J. (1972) *Semantic Theory*, New York: Harper & Row

— (1975) 'Logic and Language: An Examination of Recent Criticisms of Intensionalism' in Gunderson and Maxwell (1975)

Kay, P. (1971) 'Taxonomy and Semantic Contrast', *Language, 41*, 866-87

Kay, P. and McDaniel, C.K. (1978) 'The Linguistic Significance of the Meanings of Basic Color Terms', *Language, 54*, 610-46

Kempson, R. (1977) *Semantic Theory*, Cambridge Textbooks in Linguistics, Cambridge: Cambridge University Press

Korner, S. (1970) *Categorial Frameworks*, Oxford: Basil Blackwell

Kripke, S.A. (1972, 1980) *Naming and Necessity*, Oxford: Basil Black-

well. First published in Davidson and Harman (1972)
Kuhn, T. (1962) *The Structure of Scientific Revolutions*, Chicago: University of Chicago Press
Lakoff, G. (1971) 'On Generative Semantics' in Steinberg and Jacobovits (1971)
— (1972) 'Linguistics and Natural Logic', in Davidson and Harman (1972)
Leech, G.N. (1974) *Semantics*, Harmondsworth: Penguin Books
Lehrer, A. (1974) *Semantic Fields and Lexical Structure*, Amsterdam: North Holland Publishing Co.
Leonard, H.S. and Goodman, N. (1940) 'The Calculus of Individuals and Its Uses', *Journal of Symbolic Logic*, 5, 45-55
Lewis, D. (1972) 'General Semantics' in Davidson and Harman (1972)
Locke, J. (1690) *An Essay Concerning Human Understanding*. Abridged edn: A.D. Woozley, (ed.) (1964), London: Fontana/Collins
— (1977) *Semantics* (2 vols.), Cambridge: Cambridge University Press
McCawley, J.D. (1968a) 'The Role of Semantics in a Grammar' in E. Bach and R.T. Harms (eds.), *Universals in Linguistic Theory*, New York: Holt, Rinehart and Winston
— (1968b) 'Lexical Insertion in a Transformation Grammar Without Deep Structure', in Darden, Bailey and Davidson (1968)
— (1971) 'Where Do Noun Phrases Come From?' in Steinberg and Jacobovits (1971)
Mackie, J.L. (1976) *Problems from Locke*, Oxford: Clarendon Press
Markman, E., Horton, M. and McLanahan, A. (1980) 'Classes and Collections', *Cognition*, 8, 227-41
Mervis, C., Rosch, E. and Catlin, J. (1975) 'Relationships Among Goodness-of-example, Category Norms, and Word Frequency', unpublished manuscript
Mervis, C.B. and Roth, E.M. (1980) 'The Internal Structure of Basic and Non-basic Color Categories', *Language*, 57, 384-405
Miller, G. (1971) 'Empirical Methods in the Study of Semantics' in Steinberg and Jacobovits (1971)
Miller, G.A. and Johnson-Laird, P.N. (1976) *Language and Perception*, Cambridge, Mass.: Harvard University Press
Mourelatos, A.P.D. (1978) 'Events, Processes and States', *Linguistics and Philosophy 2*, 425-34
Nida, E.A. (1975a) *Componential Analysis of Meaning*, The Hague: Mouton
— (1975b) *Exploring Semantic Structures*, München: Wilhelm Fink Verlag

Norman, D.A. and Rumelhart D.E. (eds.) (1975) *Explorations in Cognition*, San Francisco: Freeman
Osherson, D.N. and Smith, E.E. (1981) 'On the Adequacy of Prototype Theory as a Theory of Concepts', *Cognition, 9*, 35-58
Peranteau, P.M., Levi, J.N. and Phares, G.C. (eds.) (1972) *Papers from the 8th Regional Meeting of the Chicago Linguistic Society*, University of Chicago: Department of Linguistics
Platts, M. de B. (1979) *Ways of Meaning*, London: Routledge and Kegan Paul
Posner, M.I. and Keele, S.W. (1968) 'On the Genesis of Abstract Ideas', *Journal of Experimental Psychology, 77*, 353-63
Pulman, S.G. (1977) 'Formal Grammar and Language Use — Their Interaction in the Analysis of Modals'. Unpublished Phd. dissertation: University of Essex.
Putnam, H. (1962) 'The Analytic and the Synthetic' in H. Feigl and G. Maxwell (eds.), *Minnesota Studies in the Philosophy of Science III*, Minneapolis: University of Minnesota Press. Reprinted in Putnam (1975a)
— (1970) Is Semantics Possible? in H.E. Kiefer and M.K. Munitz (eds.), *Language, Belief and Metaphysics*, New York: State University of New York Press. Reprinted in Putnam (1975a)
— (1975a) *Mind, Language and Reality: Philosophical Papers Vol. 2*, Cambridge: Cambridge University Press
— (1975b) 'The Meaning of Meaning' in Gunderson and Maxwell 1975. Reprinted in Putnam (1975a)
— (1978) *Meaning and the Moral Sciences*, London: Routledge and Kegan Paul
— (1981) 'Quantum Mechanics and the Observer', *Erkenntnis, 16*, 193-219
Quine, W.V.O. (1960) *Word and Object*, Cambridge, Mass.: MIT Press
— (1964) *From a Logical Point of View* (2nd edn), Cambridge, Mass.: Harvard University Press
— (1969) 'Reply to Chomsky' in Davidson and Hintikka (1969)
— (1970) 'Natural Kinds' in N. Rescher (ed.), *Essays in Honor of Carl Hempel*, Dordrecht: Reidel Publishing. Reprinted in Schwartz (1977)
— (1971) 'The Inscrutability of Reference' in Steinberg and Jacobovits (1971)
— (1972) 'Methodological Reflections on Current Linguistic Theory' in Davidson and Harman (1972)
— (1974) *The Roots of Reference*, La Salle, Illinois: Open Court Publishing

— (1979) 'Facts of the Matter' in Shahan and Swoyer (1979)
Reed, S.K. (1972) 'Pattern Recognition and Categorization', *Cognitive Psychology, 3*, 382-407
— (1978) 'Schemes and Theories of Pattern Recognition' in Carterette and Friedman (1978)
Rips, L.J., Shoben, E.J. and Smith, E.E. (1974) 'Semantic Distance and the Verification of Semantic Relations', *Journal of Verbal Learning and Verbal Behaviour, 12*, 1-20
Robson, C. (1973) *Experiment, Design and Statistics in Psychology*, Harmondsworth: Penguin Books
Rosch, E.H. (1973) 'Natural Categories', *Cognitive Psychology, 4*, 328-50
— (1978) 'Principles of Categorisation' in Rosch and Lloyd (1978)
Rosch, E. and Mervis, C. (1975) 'Family Resemblances: Studies in the Internal Structure of Categories', *Cognitive Psychology, 7*, 573-605
Rosch, E.H. *et al.* (1976) 'Basic Objects in Natural Categories', *Cognitive Psychology, 8*, 382-439
Rosch, E. and Lloyd, B. (eds.) (1978) *Cognition and Categorisation*, Hillsdale, NJ: Lawrence Erlbaum Associates
Rosenberg, J.F. and Travis, C. (eds.) (1971) *Readings in the Philosophy of Language*, Englewood Cliffs, NJ: Prentice-Hall Inc.
Russell, B. (1940) *An Inquiry into Meaning and Truth*, Harmondsworth: Penguin Books (1973 edn)
Sampson, G. (1979) 'The Indivisibility of Words', *Journal of Linguistics, 15*, 39-47
— (1980) *Making Sense*, London: Oxford University Press
Schank, R.C. (1972) 'Conceptual Dependency: A Theory of Natural Language Understanding', *Cognitive Psychology, 3*, 552-631
— (ed.) (1975) *Conceptual Information Processing*, Amsterdam: North Holland
Schwartz, S.P. (ed.) (1977) *Naming, Necessity, and Natural Kinds*, Ithaca and London: Cornell University Press
— (1978) 'Putnam on Artifacts', *The Philosophical Review, LXXXVII*, 566-74
— (1980) 'Natural Kinds and Nominal Kinds', *Mind, LXXXIX*, 182-95
Searle, J.R. (1969) *Speech Acts*, London: Cambridge University Press
— (1975) 'Indirect Speech Acts' in Cole and Morgan (1975)
Seuren, P.A.M. (ed.) (1974) *Semantic Syntax*, Oxford Readings in Philosophy, London: Oxford University Press
Shahan, R.W. and Swoyer, C. (eds.) (1979) *Essays on the Philosophy of W.V. Quine*, Hassocks, Sussex: The Harvester Press

Shepard, R.N. (1962) 'The Analysis of Proximities: Multidimensional Scaling With an Unknown Distance Function I and II' *Psychometrika, 27*, 125-40; 219-46

Steinberg, D.D. and Jakobovits, L.A. (eds.) (1971) *Semantics: An Interdisciplinary Reader in Philosophy, Linguistics and Psychology*, Cambridge: Cambridge University Press

Strawson, P.F. (1959) *Individuals: An Essay in Descriptive Metaphysics*, London: Methuen

— (1961) 'Singular Terms and Predication', *Journal of Philosophy, 58* (15), 393-412. Also in Strawson (1967)

— (ed.) (1967) *Philosophical Logic*, Oxford Readings in Philosophy Series, Oxford: Oxford University Press

— (1974) *Subject and Predicate in Logic and Grammar*, London: Methuen

Turner, J. (1975) *Cognitive Development*, London: Methuen

Whorf, B.L. (1956) 'Language, Thought and Reality' in J.B. Carroll (ed.), *Selected Writings of Benjamin Lee Whorf*, Cambridge, Mass.: MIT Press

Wierzbicka, A. (1972) *Semantic Primitives*, Frankfurt: Athenaeum

Wiggins, D. (1971) 'On Sentence-sense, Word-sense and Difference of Word Sense. Towards a Philosophical Theory of Dictionaries' in Steinberg and Jacobovits (1971)

Wilks, Y.A. (1972) *Grammar, Meaning and the Machine Analysis of Language*, London: Routledge and Kegan Paul

— (1977a) *Good and Bad Arguments About Semantic Primitives*, Research Report No. 42, Department of Artificial Intelligence, University of Edinburgh

— (1977b) *Making Preferences More Active*, Research Report No. 32, Department of Artificial Intelligence, University of Edinburgh

Wittgenstein, L. (1972) *Philosophical Investigations*, trans. G.E.M. Anscombe, Oxford: Basil Blackwell. First edn (1953)

Zadeh, L. (1965) 'Fuzzy Sets', *Information and Control, 8*, 338-53

Zwicky, A. (1973) 'Linguistics as Chemistry: The Substance Theory of Semantic Primes' in Anderson and Kiparsky (1973)

INDEX

abstraction 76-8
analytic hypothesis 13, 14, 18, 22-9 *passim*
analytic specification 155-66 *passim*
Anderson, E.S. 85
Anglin, J. 64, 124-6
Austin, J.L. 108

basic category 73, 85, 89, 90, 93, 104, 105, 108, 125
Basso, K.H. 82n6
Battig, W.F. 86, 110
Benacerraf, P. 61
Bendix, E.H. 49n1
Bennett, J. 161
Berlin, B. 53, 82n6, 83, 85, 90, 107
Bever, T.G. 76, 78, 82n6
biconditional definition 41-7 *passim*, 155, 166, 167
Bierwisch, M. 49n1
Binnick, R. 45
Bolinger, D. 31
Bower, T.G.R. 58, 59
Bowerman, M. 136n2
Breedlove, D. 82n6

calculus of individuals 61-9 *passim*
category formation 53, 55, 73, 74, 77, 90-106 *passim*, 114, 168
Catlin, J. 122
Chomsky, N. 9, 18-22, 26, 29, 42, 50n2, 52, 56, 60-9 *passim*, 99, 106n1, 124, 143-7, 154, 169n1
Clark, E. 49n1
Clark, H. 49n1
Coleman, L. 133, 136n1
cross-classification 77, 78, 109, 112, 162
Cruse, D.A. 68, 82n8
cue validity 88-106 *passim*

Davidson, D. 9, 11, 24, 38, 40, 41, 46, 50n5
Dixon, R.M.W. 108
Donnellan, K. 146
Dowty, D. 50n4

entailment 16, 17, 47, 52, 75, 78, 80, 103, 106, 155
essential properties 55, 70, 140-9 *passim*, 162, 165
Evans, G. 33, 37, 39, 50n4

familiarity 123-7
family resemblance 91, 92, 104, 105, 113-22, 128-32
Fillmore, C.J. 49n1
Fodor, J.A. 24, 31, 42, 44, 50n5, 51n6, 76
Fodor, J.D. 31
Foster, J.A. 50n2

Garrett, M.F. 76
Geach, P. 77
Gibson, R.F. 28, 106n1
Goodman, N. 60-2, 65
Grice, H.P. 14, 15

Harris, Z. 12
Hayes, P.J. 82n2
Hays, W. 120 note a
Hockney, D. 23, 24, 28
Horton, M. 81
Hurford, J. 82n4
hyponymy 110-12

indeterminacy of psychology 25-7
indeterminacy of translation 9-28 *passim*, 52, 93-6
indexical term 153, 154, 158, 162

Jackendoff, R. 29, 30, 34
Johnson-Laird, P. 49n1

Katz, J.J. 9, 15, 16, 29-44 *passim*, 147-9
Kay, P. 53, 75, 76, 133-5, 136n1
Keele, S.W. 124
Kempson, R. 31
Korner, S. 82n5
Kripke, S. 55, 137-43 *passim*
Kuhn, T. 35

Lakoff, G. 42, 44, 49n1, 133
Lehrer, A. 49n1
Leonard, H.S. 61

Lewis, D. 31, 32, 33
Locke, J. 76-8, 154, 161
Lyons, J. 31, 32, 60, 70, 72, 95, 106, 109

Mackie, J.L. 146, 147
markerese 33, 39-41
Markman, E. 81
mass term 70-2, 90, 153, 169
McCawley, J.D. 11, 42, 49n1
McDaniel, C. 133, 134, 135
McDowell, J. 33, 37, 39, 50n4
McLanahan, A. 81
meanings as entities 9, 12, 14, 16, 17, 30, 46, 48
Mervis, C. 86, 88, 91, 114, 122, 124, 127, 133
metaphysical necessity 140 *passim*, 156, 164
Miller, G. 46n1, 84
Montague, W.E. 86, 110
Mourelatos, A. 169

nameable object 53-78 *passim*, 101, 102, 168
natural kind word 10, 55, 96, 137-59 *passim*
Nida, E.A. 49n1
nominal kind word 154-66 *passim*
Norman, D.A. 49n1

observation sentences 12, 22
one-criterion words 15, 154, 164
Osherson, D. 134, 135, 136n4

physical object 13, 27, 52, 56-62, 73, 75, 81, 93-9
Platts, M. 39
Posner, M.I. 124
primary kind word 161-6 *passim*
proper name 53, 55, 60, 66, 74, 137, 138, 143, 146
prototype 87-106 *passim*, 107-36 *passim*, 150, 151
Putnam H. 9, 15, 16, 25, 26, 42, 49, 55, 61, 137-43, 148-58 *passim*

Quine, W.V.O. 9-33 *passim*, 42-8 *passim*, 57, 60, 71, 73, 77, 93-6, 101, 106n1, 138

Raven, P. 82n6
Reed, S.K. 88, 124
Rips, L.J. 127, 128, 130

Rosch, E. 53, 71, 86-106 *passim*, 107-36 *passim*
Rosenbaum, P. 78, 82n8
Roth, E.M. 133
Rumelhart, D.E. 49n1
Russell, B. 63

Sampson, G. 9, 31, 65-8
scattered objects 60-9 *passim*, 81
Schank, R. 49n1
Schwartz, S.P. 139, 154-66 *passim*, 169n1
Searle, J.R. 46, 47, 137
semantic category 54-6, 137-69 *passim*
semantic markers 30, 32, 33, 43, 151-3
semantic metatheory 23-9 *passim*
semantic primes 35-8, 41
semantic primitives 30, 31, 44
semantic similarity 127-32, 151
shared beliefs vs. meanings 10-12, 15-17, 46, 48, 80, 136
Shepherd, R.N. 127
Shoben, E.J. 127, 128
Smith, E.E. 127, 128, 134, 135, 136n4
stable generalisation 156-66 *passim*
stereotype 141-3, 148-53, 162-8 *passim*
Strawson, P.F. 14, 15, 63, 65
subordinate category 89, 104, 105, 125
substance 71, 74, 146, 153, 162
superordinate category 71, 89, 90, 104, 105, 109, 125
synonymy 9, 10, 17, 18, 42-7, 65, 76

Tarski, A. 38, 40
taxonomic structure 75-87 *passim*, 107-9, 112
translation manual 12-27 *passim*, 29
truth theory 37-41, 50n5
Turner, J. 59

universal grammar 55, 168

Whorf, B.L. 53
Wierzbicka, A. 42
Wilks, Y. 49n1
Wittgenstein, L. 56, 59, 91

Zadeh, L. 133
Zwicky, A. 35-8

For Product Safety Concerns and Information please contact our EU
representative GPSR@taylorandfrancis.com
Taylor & Francis Verlag GmbH, Kaufingerstraße 24, 80331 München, Germany

www.ingramcontent.com/pod-product-compliance
Lightning Source LLC
Chambersburg PA
CBHW070402240426
43661CB00056B/2508